TWO TOGETHER

Anthology

SERIES EDITORS
Margaret Iveson
Samuel Robinson

EDITORIAL CONSULTANT
Alan Simpson

LITERATURE CONSULTANT
Rivka Cranley

TEACHER CONSULTANTS
Flora Miller
David Crichton
Judy Thorne

PRENTICE HALL CANADA INC.

ISBN 0-13-020173-1

Anthologists: Todd Mercer, Linda Sheppard
Researchers: Monika Croydon, Catherine Rondina

A Ligature Book
Cover Photograph: © Dale Sanders/Masterfile

Canadian Cataloguing in Publication Data
Main entry under title:

Working Together: anthology

(MultiSource)
ISBN 0-13-020173-1

1. Cooperation–Literary collections. 2. Work–Literary collections.
3. Children's literature. I. Iveson, Margaret L., 1948– .
II. Robinson, Sam, 1937– . III. Series.
PZ5.W67 1993 j808.8'0355 C92–095205–4

Printed and bound in Canada

When you cease to make a contribution,

you begin to die.

ELEANOR ROOSEVELT

(1884–1962)

Contents

One Thousand Cranes

There is an old Japanese legend
that making a thousand cranes
folding them from coloured paper
allows the maker to have any wish
come true—at least anything reasonable
Surely it was not unreasonable
for a little girl to wish to live
as Sadako Sasaki did wish
tho ill of "radiation disease"
since The Bomb fell on Hiroshima
Sadako folded 643 paper cranes
but never reached a thousand
and died in October 1955
at the age of 12
In Hiroshima near ground zero
of the atomic holocaust
Japanese schoolchildren across the country
built a monument to Sadako
and all those other dead children
From Hokkaido to far Kyushu
the children saved their yen
to build the Statue of the A-Bomb Children
with Sadako standing on top
still folding her paper cranes
as she did in life

When I visited the statue today
Sadako was there
and underneath in a sort of alcove
thousands and thousands of paper cranes
folded by the living children of Japan
For Sadako and all those others
the dead children of Hiroshima
The crane legend is very old
and certainly it isn't true
that if you fold a thousand cranes
Kwannon the god of children
will cool the radiation fever
And intercede with death for a child
Perhaps the Japanese schoolchildren
never believed the legend of a thousand cranes
but whether they believed it or not
they acted as if they did
and built the monument
—that seems important

HIROSHIMA

AL PURDY

Celebration

I shall dance tonight.
When the dusk comes crawling,
There will be dancing
    and feasting.
I shall dance with the others
    in circles,
        in leaps,
            in stomps.
Laughter and talk
    will weave into the night,
Among the fires
    of my people.
Games will be played
And I shall be
    a part of it.

ALONZO LOPEZ

Pickling Beets

Why don't you peel the skins off first?
Let the water do the work.
They're too hot to touch.
Cut them under cold running water.
How small?
Just so they'll fit through the mouths.
What makes them so red?
They are blood, the blood of the earth.
The steamy vinegar makes me cry.
Let a tear fall into the kettle.
Is the fire right?
More pine will make it burn hot and quick.
Can I pour the spice?
Yes, just to the top of the curve of the belly.
I spilled some.
Wipe the mouths with this soft diaper.
Do beets feel, Nana?
Of course they do, they bleed when they boil.
Why do we hurt them?
To eat. They understand.
Do you think they die?
No, sweetheart, they only change.
What will they taste like?
At Christmas, we'll taste August.

Can I eat some now?
No, patience is the main ingredient.
What's that sound?
They're telling us they're sealed.
Sealed from what?
Nothing can get in, not even winter.
Nana, look! Our hands are red! We look like them!
We are.

LISA MOORE

My Home Is Not Broken, It Works

From the article by Carol Kleiman

One summer day, my son Robert, then five years old, took me by the hand and asked me to go outside with him.

Holding on tightly, he carefully walked around the house with me, looking at doors and windows and shaking his head. There was something he didn't understand.

"Mommy," he finally asked, pressing my hand with his warm, chubby fingers, "is our home broken?"

His words shot through my body, alerting every protective instinct, activating my private defense system, the one I hold in reserve to ward off attacks against women and children.

"Oh, Robbie," I answered, hugging him, "did someone tell you that we have a broken home?"

"Yes," he said sweetly. "But it doesn't *look* broken!"

"It's not," I assured him. "Our house is not broken and neither are we."

I explained that "broken" is some people's way of

describing a home with only one parent, usually the mother. Sometimes there was only one parent because of divorce, like us. "There are still lots of homes like ours. And they're still homes."

Robbie looked relieved and went to play with his friends. I stood there, shaking with anger.

What a way to put down a little kid and me, too, I thought. I supported my three children, fed and clothed them. I was there for them emotionally and physically. I managed to keep up payments on the house. Although we struggled financially, we were happy and loving. What was "broken" about us?

Our Stock of Food and Clothes

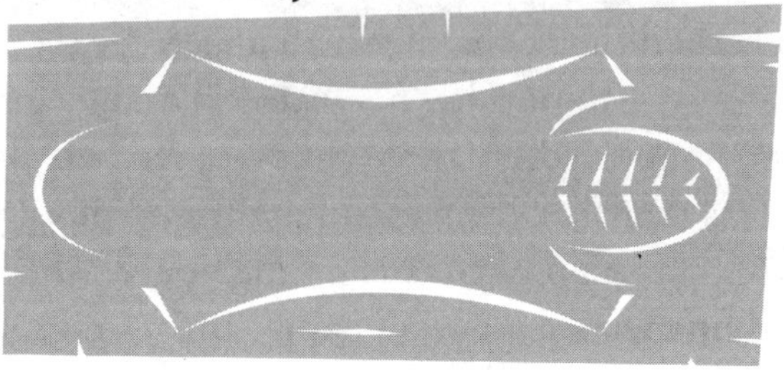

An oral account by Aleck Paul

Whites who lived alongside Aboriginal Peoples found it difficult to accept the idea that native hunters enjoyed any sense of property. They seemed to roam at will. How could they "own" land or resources as white people did? As a Chippewa man explained to anthropologist Frank G. Speck, however, his people had definite customs regarding territorial rights, which were trespassed at high cost.

Among Aboriginal groups in California, the Northwest Coast, along the Atlantic seaboard, and elsewhere as well, Aboriginal Peoples commonly recognized the inherited right to use berry patches, fishing banks, trapping or hunting grounds—sometimes marking them with visible signs such as boulders or blazed trees. The Chippewa speaker is Aleck Paul, from the Temagami band located at Bear Island, Ontario.

In the early times the Indians owned this land where they lived bounded by the lakes, and rivers, and hills, or determined by a certain number of days' journey in this direction or that. These tracts formed the hunting grounds owned and used by the different families. Wherever they went the Indians took care of the game animals, especially the beaver, just as the Government takes care of the land today.

So these families of hunters would never think of damaging the abundance or the source of supply of the game, because this had come to them from their father and grandfather and those behind them. . . .

The Indian families used to hunt in a certain section for beaver. They would only kill the small beaver and leave the old ones to keep on breeding. Then when they got too old they too would be killed, just as a farmer kills his pigs, preserving the stock for his supply of young. The beaver is the Indian's pork, the moose his beef, the partridge his chicken. And there was the caribou or red deer, that was his sheep. All these formed the stock on his family hunting ground, which would be parceled out among the sons when the owner died.

He says to his sons, "You take this part. Take care of this tract. See that it always produces enough." That was what my grandfather told us. His land was divided among two sons, my father and Pisha'bo (Tea Water), my uncle. We were to own this land so no other Indians could hunt on it. Other Indians could travel through it and go there, but could not go there to kill the beaver. Each family had its own district where they belonged and owned the game. That was each one's stock, for food and clothes.

If another Indian hunted on our territory we, the owners, could shoot him. This division of the land started in the beginning of time, and always remained unchanged. I remember about twenty years ago some Nipissing Indians came north to hunt on my father's land. He told them not to hunt beaver. "This is our land," he told them; "you can fish but must not touch the fur, as that is all we have to live on." Sometimes an owner would give permission for strangers to hunt for a certain time or on a certain tract. This was often done for friends or when neighbors had had a poor season. Later the favor might be returned.

When the white people came, they commenced killing all the game. They left nothing on purpose to breed and keep up the supply, because the white man don't care about the animals. They are after the money. After the white man kills all the game in one place, he can take the train and go three hundred miles or more to another and do the same there.

You can write this down for me. If an Indian went to the old country, England, and sold hunting licenses to the old country people for them to hunt on their own land, the white people would not stand for that. The Government sells our big game, our moose, for $50.00 license and we don't get any of it. The Government sells our fish and our islands or gets the money, but we don't get any share.

What we Indians want is for the Government to stop the white people killing our game, as they do it only for sport and not for support. We Indians do not need to be watched about protecting the game; we must protect the game or starve. We can take care of the game just as well as the game warden and better, because we are going to live here all the time. . . .

LAURA

and the LILIES

A short story by K. Reed Needles

My mother grew lilies. Not that she was the only one in the neighbourhood who did, but hers were special; perhaps because the achievement of even four or five blooms in the midst of an extended family of teenagers, as many as fourteen at times, was remarkable. But Mother had dozens of lilies—despite the lawn fights with the hose, the midnight horse escapes, the digging dogs. The cry comes down over the years: "Not in the lilies!!" Farm life was not gentle, especially on gardens.

She grew them for herself, tending them like children, all the while professing to not much care what happened to them eventually. But, in late summer, her pride in them allowed her to pick a few blooms and display them—on the mantel in the house, on the chancel steps or the altar at church, and at the fall fair. Once, she even had some photographed and framed.

In this she was not alone, since many of her friends

did the same; although not with the ferocity which seemed to accompany most of Mother's "good works." So a friendly rivalry grew in the neighbourhood, especially as the summer ended and the harvests in gardens and fields began to come in.

As teenagers, we thought of these gardens as a mild form of hysteria on Mother's part; and so we humoured her in helping to plant and weed and cut borders, and chase away the livestock.

For some reason, on the night in question Mother had gone to the city, leaving only two of us—my sister Laura and me—to look after the place. Why there were only two of us I forget. Momma simply said, "Keep the place standing," and left. Oh, she would be back late the next day, so there was nothing unnerving about her absence. So we did the chores, fed ourselves, talked and read and cleaned up, and then went to bed. Bed for Laura, as a girl, was upstairs in the house; I slept, like the rest of the boys, in a large open loft above the dairy and garage, next to the house. All the boys and visiting men slept there, in old army cots that lined the walls, with our clothes hanging over the rafters, and personal possessions in orange crates standing beside each bed. My brothers and I slept there until the first snowfall each year, when Mother finally relented and we were allowed back in the house.

I sleep well. Nothing short of the Last Judgment is likely to waken me before dawn. Laura, on the other hand, sleeps with one eye open; which is probably why this all happened.

The dogs started barking out on the porch. Not unusual, except that they kept at it with sufficient excitement to bring Laura out of bed and downstairs in her night-gown. She lit a lantern and went out on the porch. She couldn't really see anything, although the dogs by this time were hysterical. She put down the lantern, went back in the house to the gunrack, and pulled down the one weapon she knew how to use: an old Ithaca double-bore .12 gauge shotgun, with barrels as long as your arm. She broke it open, rummaged around in the drawer until she found two shells to fit it, loaded and snapped it shut, and went back out onto the porch. She called the dogs back, tucked the butt of the gun under her arm, cocked both barrels—and then couldn't remember which trigger drove which barrel. So she pulled them both.

I woke up.

By the time I got to the porch, the dogs were long gone. So, for that matter, was whatever she'd been shooting at. But Laura was still there. She was lying flat on her back with the wreckage of the screen-door under her, in the middle of the kitchen floor, holding aloft a smoking shotgun.

"Did I get it?" she asked, as I stepped through the rubble and retrieved the gun.

"Did I get it?" she asked as I helped her up off the floor and dusted her.

"Did I get it?" she demanded as she stood on the porch, rubbing her behind, while I surveyed the damage out in the yard.

Well, she hadn't exactly missed. She missed the midnight raider all right, whatever it was. Not a sign of it. But those two loads of heavy shot had sawn off the whole bed of Mother's lilies about twelve inches off the ground, just as neatly as if you'd run a mower over them.

Well, that was that, thought I. Hell to pay, death and destruction, grounded, loss of income, visions of handcuffs, prison, and dishes for months—we were not a happy pair as we went back to bed.

Next morning after chores, I set about rebuilding the

screen-door, still wondering what to do about those damn flowers. I was about halfway through when a car came down the lane. Out climbed Mrs. Brett, our neighbour, also our grade-school teacher. I can still recall her voice as she surveyed the carnage.

"What's happened to your door, boy, and . . . gracious, child, whatever happened to your mother's lilies!"

We began to explain, painfully. ("Well, miz Brett, Laura was shooting at a coon, least we thought it was a coon, and she missed, well she didn't miss exactly . . .") Forty years as a farm wife and teacher made Mrs. Brett a force to be reckoned with. She flapped a hand at me and I shut up. She pointed imperiously at her car. "Laura Ann, you get in that car. Boy, I want that door fixed and swinging by the time we get back!" And they drove off.

I had just finished touching up the paint when they returned. Laura got out of the car, and together she and Mrs. Brett lugged a bushel-basket from the trunk and over to the flower bed.

It was full of lilies, all colours, all varieties.

"Don't just stand there, child, fetch a bucket of water. Now Laura, we'll need a shovel . . ."

And in half an hour, we had removed the shattered stems and leaves of Mother's lilies and replaced them all, in neat rows, packed and watered, with the new ones.

We then stood for ten minutes, enduring Mrs. Brett's wrath. Ten of the worst minutes of our lives, while she recalled with painstaking detail every misdemeanour, failing, mistake, memory loss, and boneheaded action that had ever befallen us; finishing with a despairing forecast of our future prospects. Grade-school teachers have that knack, have you ever noticed? Then she left, calling "Don't tell your mother" out the window.

The flowers, according to Laura, had been donated by

the neighbours. “Donated” may be stretching it, since people seldom said no to Mrs. Brett, but she got them just the same, by twos and threes, from her own and other gardens, and brought them to us. Such was the community that raised us.

Mother came in due course. She made a fuss all right, but not about the flowers. She got green paint on her hand when she opened the screen-door, and that sort of took her mind off everything else. She did thank us for weeding her flowers though.

At the fair, Momma’s lilies took home first prize. Everyone congratulated her, which wasn’t surprising. They were everyone’s after all. But no one ever told her, then or since. To this day, I don’t think Mother ever knew those weren’t her lilies.

SALVADOR
late or early

A short story by Sandra Cisneros

Salvador with eyes the color of caterpillar, Salvador of the crooked hair and crooked teeth, Salvador whose name the teacher cannot remember, is a boy who is no one's friend, runs along somewhere in that vague direction where homes are the color of bad weather, lives behind a raw wood doorway, shakes the sleepy brothers awake, ties their shoes, combs their hair with water, feeds them milk and corn flakes from a tin cup in the dim dark of the morning.

Salvador, late or early, sooner or later arrives with the string of younger brothers ready. Helps his mama, who is busy with the business of the baby. Tugs the arms of Cecilio, Arturito, makes them hurry, because today, like yesterday, Arturito has dropped the cigar box of crayons, has let go the hundred little fingers of red, green, yellow, blue, and nub of black sticks that tumble and spill over and beyond the asphalt puddles until the crossing-guard lady holds back the blur of traffic for Salvador to collect them again.

Salvador inside that wrinkled shirt, inside the throat that must clear itself and apologize each time it speaks, inside that forty-pound body of boy with its geography of scars, its history of hurt, limbs stuffed with feathers and rags, in what part of the eyes, in what part of the heart, in that cage of the chest where something throbs with both fists and knows only what Salvador knows, inside that body too small to contain the hundred balloons of happiness, the single guitar of grief, is a boy like any other disappearing out the door, beside the schoolyard gate, where he has told his brothers they must wait. Collects the hands of Cecilio and Arturito, scuttles off dodging the many schoolyard colors, the elbows and wrists crisscrossing, the several shoes running. Grows small and smaller to the eye, dissolves into the bright horizon, flutters in the air before disappearing like a memory of kites.

Farm baseball

After supper we play
ball in the yard
embraced by the shadows
of gathering dusk

My cousin wears
a John Deere cap, the one
his father might have worn
in a previous game

The children giggle:
it's them against us
as it was 20 years before
small nervous offspring
testing their uncertain powers
on a makeshift diamond
shoes & chairs for bases

Dad hits a long fly
into the tall trees
that sprang from saplings
one Sunday long ago
He pauses for a moment
to savour the ball's high
c
e t
j o
a r
r y
t
thru the clean August air

The adults move to make
a play on my son
"Get him get him!" cries my mother
reliving the time
she tried to catch
my dodgy youth

A doubleplay:
my aunt waits at 1st
with outstretched arms
to tag her daughter—
the two of them lost
in private ecstasy

Like 20 years before though
the sky turns to velvet
& the grown-ups tire first
The children plead for
extra innings
but "umpires" have deaf ears

Played out, we all retire
from the field
our ritual of the summer lawn
postponed because of dark

Walking toward our twilight cars
we dream of being around
in time for the next
unscheduled game

RICHARD DAVIES

The Phantom Dog Team

A short story by Harry Paddon

All sparsely populated back country areas have their ghosts and Labrador, like the rest, has its share. The nice thing about the ghosts of Labrador is that they have kept the qualities of the old-timers of the era in which they entered the spirit world. They are a friendly, helpful group of spirits with more constructive things to do than merely to haunt the living as their more highly civilized counterparts seem to do. Instead, they appear to have a protective attitude towards their still living neighbors and descendants.

Such a one is the "Smoker" who, many times, has stuck his ethereal nose into the battering blasts of a Labrador blizzard to rescue a careless or unlucky traveller who should have known better.

How the Smoker got his name I couldn't say unless it derives from his ability to appear and vanish like a puff of smoke, or possibly it came from the fact that his appearance always occurred on a night of smoking thick drift on the barren lands he ranged. There is no question that the many to whom he appeared, including a newly-arrived and hard-boiled Hudson's Bay man who had never heard of him, firmly believe that he did indeed come to their aid and that without his help they would surely have perished. The particular incident I wish to relate occurred some 50 years ago and, since the people involved were friends of my family, I shall take a few liberties with their names though the story shall remain theirs as they told it.

Bill and Jane Gordon's winter home lay several miles inland from their summer fishing place at Bluff Head. Chosen for the generous area of woods that had furnished logs for the comfortable house and now sheltered it from the savage winds off the rocky barrens, the winter place was an isolated spot. The nearest neighbors were two families at Rocky Cove, 15 miles across the barren, rocky neck, and it was nearly 40 miles to the trading post at Rigolet. The Neck was something to be treated with respect by winter travellers, for the way across the bare, windswept ridges was unmarked and to go astray in one of the frequent winter gales was to risk death by freezing on its pitiless miles of shelterless rocks and ice, or by plunging storm-blinded from one of its many cliffs.

A few days before Christmas Bill and Jane left home to go to Rigolet to trade their furs and bring home a few extras from the store. The two children, 12-year-old Joe and little Janet, 10, were undismayed at the prospect of being left to fend for themselves for a night or two. Joe had considered himself a man for quite some time, for he could do a man's work in the woods or the fish stage, and he had been hunting and trapping alone for a couple of winters. Janet reckoned she could look after the house as well as any woman. Joe, as he helped his father harness the dogs that morning, was rather looking forward to being the boss for a while, and it was with quite a holiday feeling that the youngsters watched the team fade into the distance as they speculated on what wonders its load might contain when it again came over the hill in two or three days.

A couple of hours on the easy going of the firm, wind-packed snow of the ridges brought Bill and Jane to Rocky Cove where they stopped briefly for a cup of tea and a yarn with the first of their neighbors that they had not seen for two months. From Rocky Cove the way lay mostly on the ice to Rigolet and their arrival there was before sundown. Putting up at the Hudson's Bay Company's kitchen, where open house was kept for travellers, they spent the evening visiting the few households of the tiny village and the next day settled to their trading. By the time this was finished it was too late to leave Rigolet and a second night was spent in the cheery company of friends who had not been seen for months and might not again be seen for many more. It was in the graying dawn of their third day from home that Bill lashed up his load and harnessed his team for the return trip.

When the red rim of the sun turned the sea ice to a crimson plain at the purple-shadowed feet of the hills they were five or six miles on their way. The day promised to be fair as the frosty vapor from the panting breaths of the dogs hung in the still air. They stopped again for a brief warm-up and a snack at Rocky Cove before starting the last 15 miles across the neck to home. It was with a slight feeling of unease that Bill noticed the beginning of a wispy cloud formation to the eastward as they pulled away from Rocky Cove and began the ascent to the ridges. The evening was calm and fine, however, and he reckoned that the two-hour run to home would be safely done long before any bad weather moved in.

The only worrisome thing was that his was a young team and the year-old pup he was training to be a leader seemed to have little sense. The old leader that had died last fall could have been trusted to take them home no matter how thick the weather, without deviating a whisker's length from the trail. Bill didn't quite know if he could trust the pup who always seemed to want to be told where to go. It was clouding in rapidly now and though still calm the very stillness held the menace of something waiting to pounce.

Halfway across the neck the first few snowflakes began to fall, and as darkness curtained the rocky slopes the first searching fingers of icy wind stirred the gathering powder into feathery swirls and dragged them, rustling, across the tops of the drifts. In the space of a quarter of an hour it was blowing a gale and in the black of the night the thickening snow blotted everything from sight in a weaving wall of wind and pelting icy particles. The team faltered, slowed and stopped. The young leader had no confidence in his ability to stay on the trail, and his mates shared his uncertainty. Unable to see more than a few yards, Bill began to consider the advisability of finding a hollow sheltered enough to burrow into the snow for the night. Though this would mean a risk of freezing, it might present a better chance of survival than would be offered by blundering blindly on with a very good chance of plunging over a cliff. Already the biting wind was beginning to leave little spots of frost bite on any exposed skin and it wouldn't be too long before Bill and Jane began to freeze quite badly.

Bill knew that they were still on the trail, for just there by his leader a pyramid-shaped cairn of rocks marked where the Big Brook trail came in from the north to join their own. He walked out through the team and stood by the cairn, recalling to mind the various folds in the nearby land that might offer shelter enough to permit them to get through this night. As he stood, the voice of another driver reached his ears, the voice of a man urging his team onward, and, as he looked, a team surged out of the swirling darkness. Nine black and white dogs trotted by almost near enough to touch. On the komatik[1] behind them knelt a lone man who gestured urgently at Bill to follow before he turned again to face his team. Bill's own dogs, crazy with excitement, were already lunging into their traces and as the komatik slid by him he dropped to his seat on the load. Though the other team was a strange one to him the driver seemed to know where he was going, for he drove with the assurance of a man whose leader had been over the road before.

For an hour the two teams trotted steadily through the swirling blackness, Bill's young team straining against their heavy load to let the young leader keep his nose almost touching the stern of the leading komatik. On some of the steeper grades where the weight of their load threatened to cause them to fall behind, the black team slowed a little to let them keep up. Bill marvelled at the control the stranger had over his team, for he was travelling light and could easily run them out of sight in no time. It wasn't till a faint spark of light through the storm showed where the house lay ahead that the strange team drew ahead in a burst of speed.

Back at the house the youngsters had been having a grand time. Joe had had one day hunting ptarmigan on the ridges above the house. The second day he had harnessed up his own team of pups and gone out to the summer place, where a day on the ice foot by the open sea had

---

1 **komatik:** an Inuit sled

yielded some of the big eider ducks that make a fine Christmas dinner. Both days, with her housework done, Janet had spent some hours fishing through the ice at the mouth of the brook, and several dozen trout and a few hundred smelt had been added to the stock of frozen fish in the bins of the storehouse. The third day they both stayed close to home, and from noon on many were the glances they took at the trail from the hills where their parents' team should appear any time now. The first twinges of anxiety began as the weather worsened at dusk. The coming of full darkness brought with it a wind that roared off the hills and drove icy scuds of drift rattling across the window panes. The youngsters were silently thoughtful as they sat down to supper. Both hoped that the storm had struck on the other side of the neck early enough to cause their parents to stay the night at Rocky Cove.

Supper was barely over when a chorus of welcoming yelps and howls from Joe's pups brought them to their feet to stare through the windows. A team, not their father's, but a team of nine big black and white dogs, drew up to the door and stopped at a low-voiced command from the driver. Joe hastily pulled on his jacket and cap to go out and welcome the stranger and Janet watched as the dogs, in the usual fashion of a team glad to have reached the end of a hard day, rolled and rubbed their faces in the snow to rid their eyes of the accumulation of frost from their breaths. The driver stood for a moment by his komatik and coiled up his long whip as he waited for some sign from within.

As Janet watched, Joe appeared from the lean-to porch and walked into the square of lamplight from the window. The leader, a huge, powerful-looking beast, gambolled playfully toward him and Joe stooped to pull its harness off. As he reached for the leader Joe stopped and gazed unbelieving at his hands, for there was nothing between them. There on the wind-swept deck he was alone, more alone than he had ever been in his life, for nine big dogs with their driver and the big tripping komatik had vanished. Joe turned and started back to the door, worried by what little Janet, watching from the window, might be making of this. As he reached for the latch-string an uproar of welcome again broke from his team of pups tethered in the edge of the woods. This time, as he turned to face whatever might be coming, it was his father's familiar team that trotted jauntily on to the lamp-lit deck.

The dogs crowded around Joe, rubbing their bodies against his legs, each frantic to draw his attention and be the next unharnessed. It wasn't till Joe had sorted out and coiled up the mass of sealskin traces that he approached the komatik to help his father unleash and carry in the load. As he straightened from his bent position to coil the long lash-line Bill asked, "What became of the team that came in ahead of us?"

Joe hoisted a heavy sack to his shoulder and turned toward the house. "There was no team," he answered quietly.

Four Men and a Box

A short story by Leslie Gordon Barnard

They came from the primordial[1] jungle, four gaunt specimens of the human race, walking as men might walk in their sleep, or before a taskmaster whose lash drives them on to the limit of their endurance. Their beards were matted, their skin full of sores, and the leeches had sucked their blood.

They hated each other with the hatred of men bound by a duty, confined by the green walls of a jungle. They hated still more, as time went on, the thing they carried; but they bore it as if it were an ark of the covenant and their God was a jealous God.

"We got to get Markgraff's stuff through," they said. "He was a good guy. We promised him."

Of the reward at the journey's end they said nothing; but each man mumbled of it in his own mind, in his own way.

1 **primordial:** primitive; existing from the beginning

They had gone with Markgraff into his green hell because he paid them well in advance. Now he was dead and they were living. Death had struck him down—some swift tropical disease had ended this geologic madness of his.

They would have understood the whole thing better if his quest had been for gold. But Markgraff had said, smiling: "There are substances which science has found to be more precious than gold." At the end they thought Markgraff had failed, that all he'd found in the jungle was Death. But it seemed otherwise; the box he gave them to take back was heavy. He'd made it himself, roughly hewn. And with the secrecy of the scientist he'd packed and sealed it when he knew he, himself, was doomed.

"It will take four of you to tote it—two at a time," Markgraff had told them.

"There are four of us," said Barry, the student.

"You'll have to spell[2] each other," Markgraff directed. "I want every man to promise me that he'll stick with it until it's safely delivered. You'll find the address on top. What you have there, if you deliver it to my friend Professor MacDonald at the coast, is more precious than gold. You won't fail? I can assure you that you'll be rewarded."

They promised him because he was a dying man and they respected him. His personality had held them together when, a score of times, with the jungle's vast monotony eating into them, they might have quarreled fatally.

Then Markgraff had smiled at them, and died. He did it quietly, as he did all things—this elderly scientist, this man who'd bound them to him by ties of intangible strength. They buried him in the heart of the jungle, baring their heads, and Barry, the student, spoke brief, remembered words of committal.[3] Even as the clods fell,

---

2 **spell:** relieve, by taking turns
3 **committal:** service for the delivery of a body to the grave

the jungle loomed larger, more menacing. Each man felt a shrinking of his own stature, a terrible aloneness, a doubt of his fellows, a suspicion that, with Markgraff gone, it would be every man for himself.

They were a curious assortment: Barry, the spectacled student; McCready, the big Irish cook; Johnson, the down-and-out, the bum Markgraff had enticed out of a water-front tavern to follow him; and Jim Sykes, the sailor, who talked a lot about home but never went there.

Sykes had the compass and map, which, when they stopped to rest, he would get out and study. He put a stubby finger on it and said, "There's where we've got to get to." It looked easy—on the map. . . .

The jungle deepened about them. They missed Markgraff, who no longer could encourage them with an optimism that was usually justified, who could find in an almost impenetrable tangle some logic for going forward. At first they talked with each other, the sound of their voices important to them. . . . Soon speech became only anathema[4] against the weight they carried, as they toted Markgraff's box through the forest. . . . Then silence fell on them, and then something worse than silence.

Longing for his water-front tavern as a parched soul in Inferno[5] might yearn for water, Johnson began to find that sudden possibilities opened to him, on the right hand or the left, tempting him. McCready's face grew sullen and dark; he kept repeating, "I'm goin' my own way. I'm not traveling with this outfit any more. I guess I've got the guts to make it." And he would cast a brooding speculative eye on the map to which Sykes, the sailor, clung.

As for Sykes, he developed a closed-in horror of this jungle, this high-walled man-trap. He wanted the sea. He

4 **anathema:** a curse
5 **Inferno:** hell

demanded horizons. He mumbled about it in his sleep, and by day he cursed the death that lay where grotesque insects and reptiles waited for the unwary. He spoke of his home, and how for years he'd meant to get back to the missus and kids—and now never would.

Barry, the student, said little, but there was a girl of whom he was thinking. He'd lie sleepless, tormented by insects, tormented by a face that at times, as happens with the faces of those dear to us, refused at this distance to come clearly into focus. To think of her was to think of a campus, green with spring and russet with autumn; of a sports field, and classrooms, and a library; of dances and moonlit walks, and a sweet, tearing good-by.

Sometimes one or another of them would pray—call out in a way that the insensitive might think was cursing; He had made this fierce jungle, these incredible trees, these flowers so large that they seemed to reduce man to a pigmy. But the mind of man cannot quarrel with Nature successfully; so it turns on its own kind. There had been bickerings and quarrels even when Markgraff was with them, but his personality, and his cause—which had become their cause—had muted quarrels.

Now, there was only Markgraff's box, growing heavier as their strength grew less. It was real—when everything else had become a mental haze. It held their bodies when their minds rebelled. It chained them when they would have split apart. Turn and turn about—this routine held them; two men alone would long since have abandoned the thing.

They hated it as a prisoner hates his chains, but they carried it as they'd promised Markgraff they would.

They watched each other, covertly,[6] lest any come near

---

[6] **covertly:** secretly

the sacred thing except to lift and bear it another mile.

Then came a day when—suddenly—as by a miracle—the forest opened.

"Glory!" Sykes cried. "We made it." He took out the map, and putting his cracked lips to it, he kissed it.

"Yes," Johnson breathed, his eyes queer, and no quarrel now on his lips. He even slapped McCready, the cook, on the back and they laughed with strange hysterical laughter. . . .

When they lifted their load again, it seemed lighter, but only for a while. They were weak now, because safety was in sight and their job all but done. But eventually the four of them bore it up a street, while natives and a few others stared at them. All four men now were staggering with exhaustion.

All they asked was to deliver it, and have done.

And yet, when they asked for a Professor MacDonald—and they found him to be a withered man in a crumpled white suit—there was a triumph in them for a moment rising above emotions, the glory of a thing shared.

When they had rested, Professor MacDonald gave them food, and they told him of their promise.

It was Johnson who, running his tongue thirstily across his lips, spoke of the reward.

The old man spread his hands in a gesture of inadequacy. "I have nothing," he said, "not a thing to reward you with except my thanks. Markgraff was my friend. He was a clever man. He was more than clever, he was a good man. You have kept faith with what he asked. I can only thank you."

Derisively Johnson stared at him. "In the box," he said hoarsely.

"The box," echoed Sykes eagerly.

"Now—you're talking," McCready said.

"Open it," they demanded. They put their joint strength to it, prying off layer after layer. McCready began to curse. "All that weight, all that carrying," he complained, and Johnson said, "Wood, and more wood. What kind of a joke is that?"

But Sykes said, "Something is there. I heard it rattle. I heard it when we walked. Look, you're through to it." They all drew close, their minds leaping, remembering the substances which science had unearthed and harnessed, beyond money and beyond price; they stared at the old man when he took the loose bits of rock in his hands, and let them drop. "Worthless," he said, puzzled, trying to feel his way into Markgraff's mind.

"Worthless!" said Sykes dully.

Then McCready, the cook, exploded. "I always thought that guy was nuts. Telling us what was in the box was worth more'n gold."

"No," Barry said quickly. "I remember his exact words. What he told us was, 'What you have there, if you deliver it to my friend Professor MacDonald at the coast, is more precious than gold.'"

"So what?" shouted McCready.

"Yeah, so what?" echoed Jim Sykes, the sailor. "I could do with some ruddy gold myself."

Johnson ran his tongue along his dry lips.

Barry looked at them all: at McCready, the big Irish cook; at Sykes, the sailor, who might some day go home; at Johnson, the water-front bum.

Then he thought of a campus, green with spring, and of a girl who waited; he thought of the jungle from which they had come—the green torment in which many a man, wandering alone, was now only a heap of whitened bones; and he thought of the dogged resolution which had made four men fight through together to keep a promise, four men held together only by this common cause. This had been Markgraff's gift to them.

"He said we'd be rewarded," Johnson whined. "I heard him say it, myself. Now what do we get out of it?"

Barry turned on him quickly. "Our lives," he said. "That's what we get—our lives—for what they are worth."

Brother Leon

A short story by Robert Cormier

Brother Leon was getting ready to put on his show. Jerry knew the symptoms—all the guys knew them. Most of them were freshmen and had been in Leon's class only a month or so, but the teacher's pattern had already emerged. First, Leon gave them a reading assignment. Then he'd pace up and down, up and down, restless, sighing, wandering through the aisles, the blackboard pointer poised in his hand, the pointer he used either like a conductor's baton or a musketeer's sword. He'd use the tip to push around a book on a desk or to flick a kid's necktie, scratching gently down some guy's back, poking the pointer as if he were a rubbish collector picking his way through the debris of the classroom. One day, the pointer had rested on Jerry's head for a moment, and then passed on. Unaccountably, Jerry had shivered, as if he had just escaped some terrible fate.

Now, aware of Leon prowling ceaselessly around the

classroom, Jerry kept his eyes on paper although he didn't feel like reading. Two more periods. He looked forward to football practice. After days of calisthenics, the coach had said that probably he'd let them use the ball this afternoon.

"Enough of this crap."

That was Brother Leon—always trying to shock. Using words like crap and bull and slipping in a few damns and hells once in a while. Actually, he did shock. Maybe because the words were so startling as they issued from this pale and inoffensive looking little man. Later on, you found out that he wasn't inoffensive, of course. Now, everyone looked up at Leon as that word crap echoed in the room. Ten minutes left—time enough for Leon to perform, to play one of his games. The class looked at him in a kind of horrible fascination.

The brother's glance went slowly around the room, like the ray of a lighthouse sweeping a familiar coast, searching for hidden defects. Jerry felt a sense of dread and anticipation, both at the same time.

"Bailey," Leon said.

"Yes, Brother Leon." Leon *would* pick Bailey: one of the weak kids, high honor student, but shy, introverted, always reading, his eyes red-rimmed behind the glasses.

"Up here," Leon said, finger beckoning.

Bailey went quietly to the front of the room. Jerry could see a vein throbbing in the boy's temple.

"As you know, gentlemen," Brother Leon began, addressing the class directly and ignoring Bailey completely although the boy was standing beside him, "as you know, a certain discipline must be maintained in a school. A line must be drawn between teachers and students. We teachers would love to be one of the boys, of course. But that line of separation must remain. An invisible line, perhaps, but still there." His moist eyes gleamed. "After all, you can't see the wind but it's there. You see its handiwork, bending the trees, stirring the leaves . . ."

As he spoke, he gestured, his arm becoming the wind, the pointer in his hand following the direction of the wind and suddenly, without warning, striking Bailey on the cheek. The boy leaped backward in pain and surprise.

"Bailey, I'm sorry," Leon said, but his voice lacked apology. Had it been an accident? Or another of Leon's little cruelties?

Now all eyes were on the stricken Bailey. Brother Leon studied him, looking at him as if he were a specimen under a microscope, as if the specimen contained the germ of some deadly disease. You had to hand it to Leon—he was a superb actor. He loved to read short stories aloud, taking all the parts, providing all the sound effects. Nobody yawned or fell asleep in Leon's class. You had to be alert every minute, just as everyone was alert now, looking at Bailey, wondering what Leon's next move would be. Under Leon's steady gaze, Bailey had stopped stroking his cheek, even though a pink welt had appeared, like an evil stain spreading on his flesh. Somehow, the tables were turned. Now it seemed as if Bailey had been at fault all along, that Bailey had committed an error, had stood in the wrong place at the wrong time and had caused his own misfortune. Jerry squirmed in his chair. Leon gave him the creeps, the way he could change the atmosphere in a room without even speaking a word.

"Bailey," Leon said. But not looking at Bailey, looking at the class as if they were all in on a joke that Bailey knew nothing about. As if the class and Leon were banded together in a secret conspiracy.

"Yes, Brother Leon?" Bailey asked, his eyes magnified behind the glasses.

A pause.

"Bailey," Brother Leon said. "Why do you find it necessary to cheat?"

They say the hydrogen bomb makes no noise: there's only a blinding white flash that strikes cities dead. The noise comes after the flash, after the silence. That's the kind of silence that blazed in the classroom now.

Bailey stood speechless, his mouth an open wound.

"Is silence an admission of guilt, Bailey?" Brother Leon asked, turning to the boy at last.

Bailey shook his head frantically. Jerry felt his own head shaking, joining Bailey in silent denial.

"Ah, Bailey," Leon sighed, his voice fluttering with sadness. "What are we going to do about you?" Turning toward the class again, buddies with them—him and the class against the cheat.

"I don't cheat, Brother Leon," Bailey said, his voice a kind of squeak.

"But look at the evidence, Bailey. Your marks—all *A*'s, no less. Every test, every paper, every homework assignment. Only a genius is capable of that sort of performance. Do you claim to be a genius, Bailey?" Toying with him. "I'll admit you look like one—those glasses, that pointed chin, that wild hair . . ."

Leon leaned toward the class, tossing his own chin, awaiting the approval of laughter, everything in his manner suggesting the response of laughter from the class. And it came. They laughed. Hey, what's going on here, Jerry wondered even as he laughed with them. Because Bailey did somehow look like a genius or at least a caricature of the mad scientists in old movies.

"Bailey," Brother Leon said, turning his full attention to the boy again as the laughter subsided.

"Yes," Bailey replied miserably.

"You haven't answered my question." He walked deliberately to the window and was suddenly absorbed in the street outside, the September leaves turning brown and crisp.

Bailey stood alone at the front of the class, as if he was facing a firing squad. Jerry felt his cheeks getting warm, throbbing with the warmth.

"Well, Bailey?" From Leon at the window, still intent on the world outside.

"I don't cheat, Brother Leon," Bailey said, a surge of strength in his voice, like he was taking a last stand.

"Then how do you account for all those *A*'s?"

"I don't know."

Brother Leon whirled around. "Are you perfect, Bailey? All those *A*'s—that implies perfection. Is that the answer, Bailey?"

For the first time, Bailey looked at the class itself, in mute appeal, like something wounded, lost, abandoned.

"Only God is perfect, Bailey."

Jerry's neck began to hurt. And his lungs burned. He realized he'd been holding his breath. He gulped air, carefully, not wanting to move a muscle. He wished he was invisible. He wished he wasn't here in the classroom. He wanted to be out on the football field, fading back, looking for a receiver.

"Do you compare yourself with God, Bailey?"

Cut it out, Brother, cut it out, Jerry cried silently.

"If God is perfect and you are perfect, Bailey, does that suggest something to you?"

Bailey didn't answer, eyes wide in disbelief. The class was utterly silent. Jerry could hear the hum of the electric clock. He'd never realized before that electric clocks hummed.

"The other alternative, Bailey, is that you are not

perfect. And, of course, you're not." Leon's voice softened. "I know you wouldn't consider anything so sacrilegious."

"That's right, Brother Leon," Bailey said, relieved.

"Which leaves us with only one conclusion," Leon said, his voice bright and triumphant, as if he had made an important discovery. "You cheat!"

In that moment, Jerry hated Brother Leon. He could taste the hate in his stomach—it was acid, foul, burning.

"You're a cheat, Bailey. And a liar." The words like whips.

You rat, Jerry thought. You bastard.

A voice boomed from the rear of the classroom. "Aw, let the kid alone."

Leon whipped around. "Who said that?" His moist eyes glistened.

The bell rang, ending the period. Feet scuffled as the boys pushed back their chairs, preparing to leave, to get out of that terrible place.

"Wait a minute," Brother Leon said. Softly—but heard by everyone. "Nobody moves."

The students settled in their chairs again.

Brother Leon regarded them pityingly, shaking his head, a sad and dismal smile on his lips. "You poor fools," he said. "You idiots. Do you know who's the best one here? The bravest of all?" He placed his hand on Bailey's shoulder. "Gregory Bailey, that's who. He denied cheating. He stood up to my accusations. He stood his ground! But you, gentlemen, you sat there and enjoyed yourselves. And those of you who didn't enjoy yourselves allowed it to happen, allowed me to proceed. You turned this classroom into Nazi Germany for a few moments. Yes, yes, someone finally protested. 'Aw, let the kid alone.'" Mimicking the deep voice perfectly. "A feeble protest, too little and too late." There was scuffling in the corridors, students waiting to enter. Leon ignored the noise. He turned to Bailey, touched the top of his head with the pointer as if he were bestowing knighthood. "You did well, Bailey. I'm proud of you. You passed the biggest test of all—you were true to yourself." Bailey's chin was wobbling all over the place. "Of course you don't cheat, Bailey," his voice tender and paternal. He gestured toward the class—he was a great one for gestures. "Your classmates out there. They're the cheaters. They cheated you today. They're the ones who doubted you—I never did."

Leon went to his desk. "Dismissed," he said, his voice filled with contempt for all of them.

Alfred the Great

A short story by Mary B. Smith

Mrs. Brown, the terror of the eighth grade, had just finished testing her last student for the day when the classroom door opened and a lanky, molasses-colored boy appeared. On his head sat a blue cap with the visor tilted rakishly over one ear. His tan shirt, at least three sizes too big, was tucked carelessly into black pants whose legs sagged like deflated balloons and crumpled over a pair of scruffy white sneakers. In one hand was an envelope.

Davida Davis gasped. "Oooh. Country done come to school."

Mrs. Brown frowned at her disapprovingly then signaled the boy with an arthritic forefinger. "Come in, sir."

The boy shuffled to a desk in front of the tiny room, where he slumped, arms folded, legs crossed at the ankles, and balefully eyed the girl sitting at the teacher's elbow.

"Seven point O. Very good," Mrs. Brown entered the score on Davida's record. "Last time it was six. Keep it up and you'll be on grade level by the end of the year."

Puffed with pride, Davida stood up. "Now I'm the best reader in the class." She picked up her bookbag, hesitated, then leaned toward the teacher and whispered behind her cupped hand, "Miss Brown, that boy live round my way. He baaad. He be cuttin' school, playin' cards and figh—."

The boy's voice rumbled deep in his chest. "You better not be talkin 'bout me, girl."

Now Mrs. Brown belonged to that genus of teacher who had no fear of young rowdies. As his tough-sounding words fell on her ears, her round, dusky face hardened; her short, grizzled hair seemed to stand up like the ruffled feathers of an agitated setting hen. She dismissed Davida with a flourish, then, eyes narrowed, she rose slowly, folded her arms and leaned toward the boy sitting across from her desk.

"Young man," she said in her deep voice, "my name is Mrs. Brown. In *this* room students do not threaten each other."

Chin raised, the boy glared at the teacher; his eyes met a piercing gaze that had deflated a thousand belligerent egos. His eyes wavered, then fell.

After a measured silence, the teacher spoke. "Now, I believe that envelope you're carrying is for me." Eyes still on the boy, she sat down. "You may bring it to my desk—after you remove your headgear."

The boy snatched off his cap. "'Scuse me. I forgot."

Mrs. Brown waved him to the chair next to her desk, opened the envelope and drew out a scribbled note: "Gerald King. 15. Disc/transf. No recs. TRUANT. Test/placement G.8."

Annoyed, she tapped the note. She had been too busy to eat and had delayed her lunch until this last period of the day. She thought of the turkey-raisin sandwich in her locker and her stomach muttered. She looked over at the sullen boy who was now staring dejectedly at the floor. A truant. If she told him to come back the next day, he might not return for weeks. And the sandwich would keep. She pushed the note under a corner of her blotter, then wrote his name on a blank 3x5 card.

"Well, Gerald, you seem to need a reading test."

"What for?" The boy's leg began to jiggle.

Nervous, Mrs. Brown wrote on the card. "We like to know something about you before we assign you to a group."

"In the other school they put me in class right away."

Without answering, Mrs. Brown handed him a book from a pile on her desk. "Read up to page five."

Opening the book as if he expected it to explode, the boy peeked in, then pushed it away. "This a baby book."

Obstinate, wrote Mrs. Brown. "Why do you think that?"

"It's skinny. And ain't nothin' but little words in it."

"The mighty oak from an acorn grew." She held out a card with ten words listed in large print. "Read these." The boy ran a shaky hand over his head. "Oh, man."

"Can't read them either, huh?" *Pre-primer,* she wrote.

He swelled up, "I can re—," then subsided beneath the teacher's steady gaze and muttered, "I just don't have my glasses, that's all. My mom got to get me some new ones."

"Tell it to the Marines." Mrs. Brown shook the strip under his nose. "Read any word you can."

The boy drew his head back and studied the words. He pointed. "*Is.*" He pointed again. "*The.* And this one's *A.*"

"Yippee." Mrs. Brown wrote the three words on the card. "When's the last time you've been to school?"

"See, I knowed that girl was talkin' about me."

Mrs. Brown tapped the slip of paper on her blotter. "This *note* says you're a truant." She wrote a problem in long division on a sheet of paper and handed it to him. "Do this." She watched the boy closely as he worked the problem.

"That was easy."

Reasoning O.K., Mrs. Brown wrote on the card. Now it was time to prick him, see if there was anything in him but hot air. She looked over at him slyly. "You say arithmetic is easy, but you can't read. Now what does that mean, that you're too dumb to do both?"

"No!" The boy's eyes flared, then cooled. "My grampa said I was smart. He the one showed me how to figure. How to drive, too."

Sensitive, she noted. "Where's your grandfather now?"

The boy shook his head sadly. "Gone." And with a little prodding, he told her about a six-year-old boy whose teen-aged mother left him on a tobacco farm in South Carolina where they were living with her parents. There was pride in his voice as he talked about helping his grandfather with the hoeing, planting and harvesting, sometimes even driving the truck to town with the crops whenever the old man got sick. "That's why he taught me how to figure. So nobody could cheat me," he said shyly. After his grandmother died, he missed a lot of school and fell behind. It seemed important for him to be with his grandfather, so he stopped going. Then two years ago, his grandfather died and he ran the farm by himself for a year. It was a tenant farm, and when the owner found out about his grandfather's death, he contacted the boy's mother. "So I had to come live with her." He sighed. "But I sure was doin' better down there than I am up here."

Determined, wrote Mrs. Brown. "You can't do better if you get kicked out of school for misbehaving."

Gerald hung his head. "Them kids laughted at the way I talk and called me 'country.' So I fighted them. But they kept on, and I kept on, so the principal sended me here."

"Every school has enough homegrown hoodlums."

"I ain't no hoodlum, ma'am." The boy spoke with quiet dignity. "Else I wouldn't be here today."

"Maybe. Or maybe you'd be in family court."

"No ma'am. I come on my own. So my mother and stepfather stop arguin' over me."

Mrs. Brown regarded the boy's scowling face, his slumped shoulder, his work-hardened hands trembling on his thighs. Her heart tightened. Her stern face softened. Now here was a boy with a logical mind, mother wit, determination. But he was caught in a web of ignorance and despair, and he might not want to be freed. Was she too late? She would find out. Face set, voice hard, she said, "Sit up, sir. Look at me."

Facing her sheepishly, the boy hitched his body up.

Mrs. Brown looked deep into his eyes and said, "You are 15 years old and you are *illiterate.*" She paused to let that awful word sink in. "You can't read. Can you?"

The boy's eyes filled. "No ma'am." His voice was husky.

Mrs. Brown almost relented, but she had trod this path for many years. Her voice was soft. "Others can." Now urgent. "Why can't you?"

The boy frowned, then pressed his lips together and stared at the floor as if he would find the answer there. At last he shrugged. "It just seem like ain't no system to it."

That answer did not surprise Mrs. Brown. Through the years she had heard similar ones. "Well there is. In fact, we have an easy one here," she paused significantly. "But a lot of kids don't want to learn it. That is, at *first.*"

The boy eyed her suspiciously. "How come?"

"They say the other kids laugh at the books they use."

"Then they stupid," snorted Gerald. "They be laughin' at 'em anyway 'cause they can't read the real books in class."

"But not for long." Mrs. Brown leaned forward. "A few years ago a boy named Alfred came here in the seventh grade. He read *worse* than you. His mother moved around a lot, so he'd been in sixteen different schools before he got to this one. He was never in one school long enough to learn how to read." Mrs. Brown tapped the book that Gerald had rejected so disdainfully a few minutes earlier. "But once Alfred learned our system, he read this book in one period."

Gerald's eyes widened. "This book?"

"Alfred piled right on through it and seven others in three months. He pulled up from reading no grade to fourth grade in half a year. And when he left here in the ninth grade, he was reading like a champ." She sat back, reminiscing. "Of course, Alfred was *smart.*"

"I could do the same thing."

"Alfred was *logical,* too. He could figure things out—" Mrs. Brown snapped her fingers—"like that."

"Me, too. And I can do arithmetic good."

"And Alfred was *determined.* He was *serious.* Once he came to school with the flu and we had to send him home."

"When grampa died, I ran the farm all by myself."

"Pooh," scoffed Mrs. Brown. "If you had stayed on that farm, you'd still be illiterate. Now when a boy gets your age," she continued, "if he wants to learn how to *read,* he has to have a thirst. Like a camel that smells water after a long trip across the blazing sands of the Sahara Desert. Learning to read is frustrating. Some days you get so mad you want to quit. Now, this boy Alfred I mentioned, he *loved* music. He wanted his own saxophone. But it cost money and his mama had three other mouths to feed. So he had to get a job. Well, the man who owned the supermarket told Alfred if he learned to read he'd give him a job. See?"

Gerald was now on the edge of his seat. "I got a good reason for learning to read, Miss!"

"You told me." Mrs. Brown closed one eye like an old hoot owl. "To stop your parents from arguing about you."

"That's why I came today." Gerald said earnestly. "But that ain't why I want to learn to read." He patted his pocket, then withdrew a small white booklet. "This the real reason." On her desk he laid a driver's manual, stained and creased from folding. "My stepfather, he fix TVs and vacuum cleaners, and he say since I can already drive, if I get my license, I might can go with him sometimes. I *got* to learn to read so I can git me a license when I turn sixteen."

Soberly, intently, tented fingers pressed against her lips, Mrs. Brown regarded Gerald like a cat watching a fledgling's first attempts at flight. "That might do."

"Please, Miss! I know I can read that book today."

Mrs. Brown eyed the clock. "We'd be here after school!" But at the boy's pleading look, she opened her desk drawer and pulled out a work packet of white squares and a set of capital letters. "I don't know." She shook her head as if in doubt. "I usually take three days with the regular kids."

Gerald hitched his chair closer to the teacher. "I'm 'a learn this system today."

Mrs. Brown placed a big red M on her desk. "First of all, letters have sounds. This is Em. Listen. "Mmmmm." She rubbed her stomach. "Like mmmm, good. Next, we blend the letters with little words." She laid a white square in front of Gerald. "The word on this card is AT." She laid the M in front of the card. "Now say the sound of Em, mmmm, then say AT." She pushed the M toward the AT card, "And you get mat."

Gerald was flabbergasted. "Like a mat in gym class?"

"A little word," said Mrs. Brown, "but it can grow. Mat. MATCH," more intensely now. "MATchable, UNmatchable!"

Gerald blinked. "Why, that's easy!" Soon he had blended most of the letters with the AT card. "What's next?"

Mrs. Brown dealt him five AT cards. "We play cards."

"Cards!"

"To reinforce what you just learned. And," she winked archly, "to spice things up a little." She dealt herself five AT cards and piled the red letters on Gerald's desk.

Then the teacher with a witch's fingers and the boy with a farmer's hands played cards. How she laughed to see that boy grunt and gasp and spit as he struggled to make lips, tongue, and teeth produce those little words.

With less effort did Hercules defeat Antaeus.

Finally Mrs. Brown tapped the book on Gerald's desk. "Read page one."

Nervously, Gerald smoothed the page. "Nat. Nat . . . is . . . ay cat." Following his long brown finger, he read as if he were walking on eggs. "Nat . . . is . . . ay . . . FAT . . . cat." He looked up. For the first time he smiled, grinning as if he had just read the first page of a Dickens novel. "He sound just like my cat. He orange and real fat. And *lazy.* You like cats, Miss Brown?"

At 3:20 Mrs. Brown was making a notation on Gerald King's card. "2/19. Read 30 pages, Book 1."

There was a light tap on the door and Davida Davis appeared in the doorway with a sheepish look on her face. “I come to say I’m sorry for actin’ up when that boy come in.”

“You’re forgiven.”

“He took a Book 1. I just seen it in his back pocket.”

Mrs. Brown chuckled. “Rolled it up, did he?”

“Yuup. When you gave me that book last year, I felt so stupid. I wasn’t gonna read it neither. Then you told me how that real smart boy named Alfred pulled up four grades in a half a year, and I said I could, too. Remember?”

Mrs. Brown smiled down at Gerald’s card. “I remember.”

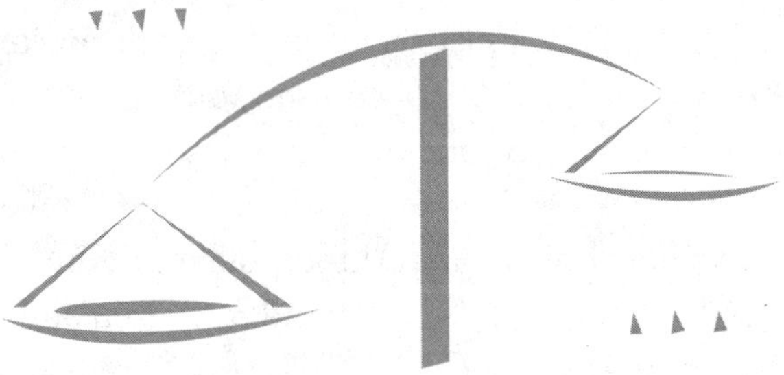

Body Politics

An edited teleplay from an episode of *Degrassi High* by Susin Nielsen

CHARACTERS

Lucy—*Bright. Aspiring film maker. Upper middle class. Has had problems in the past with her parents who tend to be too busy to spend time with her.*

Lucy's Mom

Dale—*Good-looking athlete. President of the student sports association.*

Dale's Friend

Erica—*Twin sister to Heather. Very bubbly. Good friends with Lucy.*

Heather—*Twin sister to Erica. The more cautious of the sisters. Good friends with Lucy.*

Amy—*Pretty and popular.*

Cindy—*B.L.T.'s new girlfriend. Athletic.*

A Guy

Bronco—*Good student. President of the student council.*

Alexa—*Boy crazy. At times naive. Very bubbly. Simon's girlfriend.*
Michelle—*Good friends with Alexa. Ex-girlfriend of B.L.T. Works part time and lives on her own.*
Luke
Luke's Friend
Nancy—*Very bright. Editor of* Degrassi Digest, *the school newspaper.*
B.L.T.—*Good athlete. Sensitive. Ex-boyfriend of Michelle.*
Simon—*Best friend of B.L.T. Quite naive. Alexa's boyfriend.*
Teacher
Leslie
Girls' volleyball team members
Boys' basketball team members

This episode of the television series Degrassi High *opens with Lucy, the main character, recording a videotape for L.D., her best friend. L.D., whose leukemia is in remission, is in the Caribbean with her father, and she and Lucy are keeping in touch through the videotapes they send back and forth.*

1 INT. LUCY'S BEDROOM. MORNING. "DAY 1"
Lucy *puts a cassette in the camcorder, turns it on, sits in a chair, and speaks to camera.*

Lucy: Hi, L.D. Thanks for your postcards. That was a great video.
Okay, time for the Lucy Fernandez news update:
The semiformal is only two weeks away. And almost everyone is going . . .

Note: *V/O*, or "voice over," indicates that a character's voice is heard but the character is not seen. *B/G*, or "background," indicates that a character is speaking in the background while other characters are in the foreground. *INT.* means "interior" and *EXT.* means "exterior."

Minus me, of course—the dateless wonder . . . Okay, I know I'm kind of opinionated . . . all right, mouthy . . . And I *know* I intimidate a lot of guys . . . But aren't there men out there who admire these qualities?

Mom: (*V/O*) Lucy! Shouldn't you be leaving for school now?

Lucy: Okay, Mom! (*into the camera*) I'll tune in later and tell you about everyone *else's* love life . . .

(Lucy *hits the remote and shuts off the camera.*)

2 INT. STAIRWAY. DAY *Kids come down stairs.* Dale, *a jockish senior, and a* Friend *approach.*

Dale: So, are you going to the semiformal?

Friend: I still have to get the nerve to ask out Linda. Are you taking Debbie again?

Dale: Are you kidding? We broke up last weekend. Now I'm single and available.

Friend: All right.

(Erica, Heather, *and* Lucy *follow down the stairs.*)

Erica: Luce! I finally found the perfect dress for the semi-formal. It's cut down to here and up to here . . .

Heather: Guaranteed to make a man drool or your money back.

Lucy: (*grins*) You guys have to take tons of pictures.

Heather: I wish you were coming.

Lucy: (*shrugs*) All the guys I know are going already.

Erica: Hey, I could set you up with Mike's friend, Kyle. He doesn't have a date.

Heather: No wonder—he's such a jerk! He is all hands.

Lucy: Okay—I'm not that desperate.

Amy: (*joins them*) Hey guys, don't forget volleyball practice.

Lucy: When is it?

Amy: Probably the same time as last year.

Erica: Okay.

Amy: (*leaving*) See ya.

Erica: I hope we do better than last year. We've got to win one game at least.

Heather: (*grins*) Now, now—it's not whether you win or you lose . . .

Erica, Heather, *and* Lucy: It's how you play the game.

(*Laughter. As* Erica, Heather, *and* Lucy *pass the sports desk,* Dale *turns and bumps into* Lucy, *who drops her books. Simultaneously—*)

Lucy *and* Dale: Sorry.

(*They both bend down to pick up the books. He looks at her.*)

Dale: . . . You're Lucy, right?

Lucy: (*smiling*) Right.

Dale: Uh . . . I've seen you in the halls. I'm Dale.

Lucy: Hi. I've . . . seen you, too.

Dale: (*as they stand*) Sorry about not watching where I was going.

Lucy: It's okay. I wasn't watching either.

(Dale *notices he's missing one of his books.* Lucy *has it . . .*)

Lucy: (*handing it back*) Oh, sorry.

Dale: Sorry.

(Dale *turns and bumps into* Erica.)

Erica: (*checking out* Dale) Sorry.

(*A* Guy *walks between* Dale *and* Erica.)

Guy: Excuse me.

(Dale *smiles, heads away.* Lucy, Erica, *and* Heather *watch him go.*)

Heather: I think he likes you.

Erica: Yeah, why don't you ask him?

Lucy: Are you kidding? A guy that cute's probably booked up to the year 2000.

3 INT. CORRIDOR. DAY *The bell rings to signal lunchtime.* Dale *and classmates come out of class as an announcement is heard on the PA.*

Bronco: (*PA*) Remember, the student council will be having its annual semiformal dance. Have you asked that special someone yet?

4 EXT. DEGRASSI. DAY Alexa *stands waiting in front of the school doors.* Michelle *approaches along the sidewalk.*

Alexa: (*stepping forward*) Hi.

Michelle: (*cold*) Hello.

Alexa: I was wondering if you wanted to go out sometime. Like old times—just you and me?

(Michelle *stops, looks at* Alexa.)

Michelle: . . . I've got Tuesday evening off.

Alexa: Tuesday? (*she sighs*) Simon invited me over for dinner and I . . . I can't ask him to . . .

Michelle: . . . Why did you even bother asking? Go marry him or something!

(Michelle *heads away.* Alexa *watches her go.*)

5 INT. CORRIDOR. DAY Lucy *puts a book in her locker as* Dale *approaches with a flower in hand. An announcement is heard on the PA.*

Bronco: (*PA*) The new schedule for the gym has been posted. All you jockular types, that is, anyone who is on a sports team is asked to check the main bulletin board for practice times. Thank you.

Dale: Hi, there.

Lucy: (*surprised*) Hi . . .

Dale: I was wondering . . . Are you going with anyone to the semiformal?

Lucy: Why?

Dale: I know we've just met, but—would you like to go with me? It would give us a chance to get to know each other.

Lucy: . . . Sure.

Friend: (*passing*) You coming, Dale?

Dale: (*to* Friend) Okay, just a second. (*to* Lucy) I'll talk to you later to make some arrangements, okay?

(Dale *hands her the flower he was holding.*)

Lucy: Okay.

(Dale *heads off down the hall bouncing a basketball.* Lucy *smiles and runs off in the opposite direction.*)

6 INT. FOYER. DAY Erica *and* Heather *walk down the hall discussing an English lecture.*

Erica: She was saying something about how *Jane Eyre* was the first feminist novel because . . . I think she said *Jane Eyre* was the first . . .

(Lucy, *running, catches up behind them.*)

Lucy: Guys! . . . Guys, you won't believe what just happened. Remember Dale, that really cute guy from this morning?

Heather: Yeah.

Lucy: (*showing off the flower*) He just invited me to the semiformal.

Erica: A flower? All right!

Lucy: I thought it was a cute touch.

Heather: Then we're all going. That's fantastic.

(Cindy *approaches. She seems upset.*)

Cindy: You have to come and see this. This is so unfair.

Lucy: What's wrong?

(*They follow* Cindy *to the phys-ed bulletin board.*)

Erica: I don't know.

Cindy: Girls' volleyball practices have been bumped to early morning. Before class.

Heather: I hate getting up early.

Lucy: Who's got our time?

Erica: The boys' basketball team?

Heather: Every day, all afternoon, they get the gym.

Lucy: We can't use it occasionally? How come suddenly *we* don't rate?

(*Shrugs from* Heather, Erica, *and* Cindy.)

Lucy: Come on. (*starts away*)

Heather: Where are we going?

Lucy: To talk to Ms. Mackenzie! We are going to fight this . . . Come on!

(Luke *and* Friend *approach bulletin board and spot new practice times.*)

Luke: Hey, hey, check it out. We got basketball after school now.

Friend: All right! That's the best time.

7 INT. CORRIDOR. DAY *The door to the phys-ed office opens and* Lucy, Erica, Heather, *and* Cindy *file out—angry.*

Erica: What a jerk!

Cindy: She wouldn't even listen to us.

Lucy: (*mockingly*) Because the boys' basketball team has a better chance of making the finals, they deserve all the help we can give them.

Heather: Well, of course, darling—they're *guys*, aren't they?

Cindy: You know what else Bryant told me, they're getting brand new uniforms. *And* equipment.

Lucy: What?

Heather: We can't even get our net fixed!

Erica: We should go on strike.

Cindy: Who'd notice? Most of the school doesn't even know there is a girls' volleyball team. We never get announced or written about . . .

Lucy: This place is *so* sexist.
Heather: Well, we have to do something.
Cindy: Sure, but what?
Lucy: . . . Wait a sec', I've got an idea . . .
(*The girls look at* Lucy, *who claps her hands and heads off.*)

8 INT. CORRIDOR. DAY *End-of-day announcements over the PA. Kids are leaving.*
Nancy: (*PA*) There will be a student council meeting tomorrow to be held in the cafeteria. All council members and all class reps are asked to attend.

9 INT. GYM. DAY Lucy, Cindy, Erica, Heather, *and the rest of the* Girls' *volleyball team are in gym outfits, getting out volleyballs and setting up their net.*
Erica: I can't wait to see the look on their faces.
(*The girls laugh.*)
Amy: Do we start playing when they walk in?
Heather: Yeah.
(B.L.T., Simon, *and a couple of other members of the basketball team enter—and stop.*)
Cindy: Girls, here they come.
(*The girls start volleying a ball back and forth.*)
B.L.T.: (*walking out*) Excuse me . . . Excuse me . . . Yo!!!
(*The* Girls *stop playing.*)
B.L.T.: Excuse me, what's going on?
Lucy: We're protesting. How come you guys get new uniforms, new equipment, and *our* gym time?
(*Acknowledgments from* Girls: *"Yeah, how come?" etc.)*
B.L.T.: (*shrugs*) Hey, it's not *our* fault.
Lucy: You got it just 'cause you're *guys*!
Heather: Exactly.

B.L.T.: Oh, really?
Simon: Unh . . . We can't help that.
Erica: Excuse me—but girls' teams should be treated just the same as guys' teams.

(Lucy *doesn't notice* Dale *entering the gym.*)

B.L.T.: Lucy, *we* don't make the rules around here. So why don't you girls please take down the stupid net. We'd like to practise.
Erica: Girls? You are a joke.
Lucy: Forget it. This is our gym time, not yours.
B.L.T.: Not this year, ladies.
Lucy, Erica, Heather, *and* Cindy: Ladies?!?!
Cindy: Umm . . . you're not the captain. We want to talk to the captain.
Luke: He's gonna say the same thing.
B.L.T.: Yo, Cap!
Dale: That's me.

(Lucy *is shocked—of all the guys in the school . . . As the rest of her teammates argue, she slips behind them, attempting to hide.*)

Cindy: You call that a captain?
Dale: What do you think you're doing?
Erica: We're here to protest the unfair allocation of gym time.
Dale: That's terrific. But there's nothing *we* can do. Talk to the phys-ed department.
Cindy: We already did. But they won't listen.
Erica: It's because we're girls, don'tcha know? They're so sexist.

(*Assorted moans and groans from the* Boys' *side.*)

Erica: Yes, they are.
Dale: Hey, gimme a break. This has got nothing to do with sexism!
Heather: Hunnh!

Dale: We stand a really good chance of winning this year, that's all.

Heather: How do you know we don't?

(*The* Boys' *team breaks out in laughter.*)

Dale: Nobody cares about girls' volleyball.

Erica: What!?!?

Heather: In *your* opinion nobody cares.

Erica: You're so obnoxious.

Dale: Look, just take down that net. We don't have time for this.

(*Both sides are yelling and screaming at one another.*)

Dale: (*shouting*) Boys, take down that net and let's start practice time.

(*The* Boys *attempt to pull down the net as the* Girls *frantically try to stop them.*)

Lucy: (*V/O*) . . . And the girls were screaming and the guys were screaming. It got insane in there . . .

10 INT. LUCY'S BEDROOM. DAY Lucy *talks straight to her camcorder.*

Lucy: . . . and L.D., I almost blew it. But I don't think he saw me. I'm gonna have to learn to keep my mouth shut.

Okay, okay—I can hear you already: What's wrong with standing up for what I believe in? Right? . . . Wrong.

L.D., this date is really important. I wish you could meet him—he is *so* cute. I just want him to like me.

(Lucy *shuts off the camera.*)

11 EXT. DEGRASSI. DAY. "DAY 2" Alexa *and* Simon *approach, with* Michelle *coming after them.*

Simon: Listen, me and B.L.T. were, like, thinking of renting a limo to take us all to the semiformal?

Alexa: What a great idea!

Simon: Thanks. I thought of it, actually.

(Alexa *sees* Michelle. *Trying to be friendly as* Michelle *passes—*)

Alexa: Hi, Michelle.

(Michelle *says nothing, heads away. Glum—*)

Alexa: Remember when it was us and B.L.T. and Michelle?

Simon: Sure—now it's us, B.L.T., and Cindy.

Alexa: . . . Yeah. But Michelle and I were best friends.

(Alexa *watches* Michelle *go into the school.)*

Alexa: I miss her.

12 INT. BACK FOYER. DAY Lucy *sits talking to* Heather *and* Erica.

Heather: But he knows you. You're on the student council.

Lucy: But why should Bronco do anything?

Erica: Well, 'cause Bronco's a nice guy. You've said so yourself.

Lucy: Yeah, but what can he do?

Heather: I don't know—*something.*

Erica: C'mon. Isn't it worth a try?

Lucy: Look, why doesn't one of you two do it? It was your idea.

Erica: And it was your idea to fight this thing in the first place.

(Heather *sees* Bronco *and* Nancy *walking towards them.*)

Heather: There he is.

Nancy: I made a list of the topics people want to table, in alphabetical order. And I also made copies for each of the class reps.

Heather: C'mon Lucy, please.

Erica: The whole volleyball team's counting on you.

Bronco: . . . Nancy, maybe you should get a hobby or something.

Nancy: I have lots of hobbies.

Bronco: Let's see the list. (*takes it*)

Lucy: (*gets up*) Bronco, do you have a moment?

Bronco: Sure.

Nancy: I'll see you at the meeting.

(Nancy *heads away*. Bronco *looks at* Lucy *and smiles.*)

Lucy: Some of us are kind of upset—they took the girls' volleyball team practice time and gave it to the boys' basketball team. We think it's unfair.

Bronco: Well, talk to the phys-ed department.

Lucy: We did. They won't listen to us.

Bronco: So, what do you expect *me* to do?

Lucy: I don't know—*something*. You are school president . . . And charming . . . persuasive . . . intelligent . . .

Bronco: Don't forget devastatingly handsome.

Lucy: (*laughs*) What can you do?

Bronco: Well, there's a meeting . . .

Lucy: (*V/O*) He's agreed to let us . . .

13 INT. GEOGRAPHY CLASS. DAY Lucy *enters, followed by* Erica *and* Heather.

Lucy: . . . present our case at the student council meeting today. If we can persuade them that we're right, then Bronco will talk to the principal.

Erica: All right!

Lucy: All of us can go, but only one of us can talk. So, we need a spokesperson.

Erica: You, obviously.

Heather: You're a good speaker.

Lucy: You mean I'm mouthy?
Erica: Well, ye-ah. But it's a quality we admire.

(*The* Teacher *enters, closes the door. As* Lucy, Erica, *and* Heather *head for their seats—*)

Teacher: Can everyone take their seats, please.
Lucy: Umm, I'd really rather not.
Heather: . . . Why not?
Lucy: Just, because.
Teacher: C'mon, Archie . . .

. . . Okay, everyone turn to page twenty-four, take a look at the graph. As you can see, we're going to talk about comparisons between mountainous regions . . .

14 INT. CORRIDOR OUTSIDE OF GEOGRAPHY CLASS. DAY *End of class.*

Teacher: . . . these are going to be very important points to remember. And I wanna make . . .

(*The bell rings.*)

Teacher: Okay folks, class dismissed. Remember, you're going to review chapter two. I want all the questions answered at the end of that chapter by next class.

15 INT. CORRIDOR. DAY *The bell rings. End-of-day announcements remind everyone about the student council meeting as kids emerge from classrooms.*

Nancy: (*PA*) A reminder that the student council meeting will be commencing shortly in the cafeteria. The scheduling problem with the gym will be on the agenda. All those interested, please attend.

16 INT. STUDENT COUNCIL ROOM. DAY *Some of the* Boys' *basketball team sits outside the cafeteria as* Dale *approaches.*

Dale: Yo, guys, c'mon . . . what are you waiting for—next Christmas?

(*They start filling up the cafeteria.*)

Simon: (*B/G*) This is ridiculous.

Dale: You know whose fault this is?

Simon: The twins.

Dale: Those loud-mouthed twins . . . no kidding.

(Dale *stops in front of some of the girls.*)

Dale: Oh, hey gorgeous, how's it going?

(Bronco *and* Nancy *are busy planning the meeting as the* Boys' *team greets each other.*)

Bronco: We have to do this one first.

Nancy: But we can't.

(Lucy *and* Cindy *enter, followed by* Heather *and* Erica.)

Cindy: Why do *I* have to be the spokesperson? I hate making speeches.

Lucy: You'll be fine. You're the captain, go on.

Cindy: So?

(B.L.T. *walks by them.*)

B.L.T.: Yo, baby, looking fine.

(Dale *bumps into* Lucy.)

Dale: We have to stop meeting like this.

(*As* Erica *enters, she spots* Dale.)

Erica: Nice shirt.

(*Student council secretary* Nancy *checks her watch, raps the gavel.*)

Nancy: Order. Can we please have order . . .

Dale: (*B/G*) It's tough being number one.

Nancy: Everyone? Can we please have order? . . . People . . . ?

Bronco: Shut up!!

(*Everyone goes quiet.*)

Bronco: Thank you . . . Okay—it's obvious most of us are

here because of the sports issue. So why don't we start with that first. Who's representing the boys' basketball team?

Dale: Yo.

(*The* Boys' *team cheers on their leader: "Go for it, Dale!" and "Right on," etc.*)

Bronco: Eloquent. Assume the position . . . And the girls?

Cindy: Uh, me, I guess.

(*The* Girls *cheer on* Cindy.)

Bronco: So who'd like to go first?

(Dale *raises his hand.*)

Dale: I will.

(Bronco *nods, and* Dale *stands, to applause from his teammates.*)

Heather: (*B/G*) Figures.

Dale: I think the boys' basketball team deserves good practice time.

Cindy: Why?

Dale: We did really well last year, and we stand an excellent chance at winning the city championship this year. At least.

(*Applause from the basketball team guys.* Lucy *squirms in her seat.*)

Erica: That's what you said last year and you lost.

Dale: We *need* new uniforms and equipment, so we'll look good representing the school.

(*Moans and groans from the* Girls' *side.*)

Cindy: Gimme a break.

Dale: It's good for the school's image.

(*The basketball team guys cheer.*)

Dale: And sorry, but let's face some facts—people are just more interested in guy's sports. Nobody cares about girls' volleyball.

Erica: (*B/G*) You pigheaded . . .

(*Outrage from the* Girls' *volleyball team. Applause from the basketball team guys.* Lucy *can't take it anymore, stands.*)

Lucy: Wait a minute—excuse me.

(*Everyone looks at her.*)

Lucy: Obviously people are more interested in boys' sports—you guys get more promotion than we do. *And* you get the complete support of the sports department, while we have to beg just to get a new net.

(*The* Girls *cheer as* Dale, *who's looking at her, decides to sit down.*)

Lucy: And so what if the boys' team has a better chance at winning—this is high school, not the pro leagues. I thought sports was about participating, and exercising, and having fun . . .

Dale: (*standing*) Okay now, this is getting a bit . . .

Lucy: And I think it's irresponsible for a school to uphold traditions that are out of date and prejudiced. We're tired of being treated as second-class citizens in our own school.

(*A round of cheers from the* Girls*—and some of the watching guys. Even* Nancy *is nodding.* Bronco *has a big smile. The* Boys' *basketball team guys exchange uncomfortable looks.* Lucy *tries to catch* Dale's *eye. He glares at her.*)

Bronco: (*shouting*) Can all class presidents please come up to the table for the final vote.

17 INT. LUCY'S BEDROOM. EVENING Lucy *sits in front of the camera. Flat—*

Lucy: . . . It was put to a vote, and we won. Great . . . Dale came up afterwards and told me some lame excuse about having to go to his aunt's on the night of the dance. Right . . .

So here I am—once again, the dateless wonder . . . I keep telling myself I should be proud of standing up for what I believe in. And I guess I am . . .
But, L.D. . . . ?
I really wanted to go to that stupid dance . . .

18 INT. CORRIDOR. DAY. "DAY 3" Michelle *is at her locker as* Alexa *approaches.*

Leslie: (*B/G*) Here's that book I owe you, Michelle.

Michelle: Thanks a lot, Leslie. I hope it helped.

Leslie: See ya later.

Michelle: See ya.

(Alexa *comes through the doors and over to* Michelle.)

Michelle: Go away.

Alexa: I will if you want. But if you're still free on Tuesday, maybe you could come over to my house?

Michelle: . . . What about Simon?

Alexa: Simon and I can go out any time. Besides, he doesn't own me, right?

(Michelle *looks at her. Sincere—*)

Alexa: Me and you haven't had a good gossip in a long time. I miss that.

Michelle: (*slow smile*) . . . Me, too . . .

(*They hug.*)

Michelle *and* Alexa: I'm sorry. It was my fault.

Michelle: No really, I shouldn't have treated you the way I did.

19 INT. FOYER. DAY Lucy *enters, still pretty down, when* Bronco *sees her, joins her.*

Bronco: Hi.

Lucy: Hi.

Bronco: I talked to the principal. Sorry.

Lucy: He said no?

Bronco: He says he'll consider it for next year. But this year he wants everybody behind the boys' basketball team supporting them. Sorry.

Lucy: . . . Thanks for trying.

(Lucy *walks away.* Bronco *catches her.*)

Bronco: . . . You were great at the meeting yesterday.

Lucy: Thanks.

Bronco: So . . . I guess you have a date for the dance and all . . . ?

Lucy: I don't go to dances.

Bronco: No? Then I guess you wouldn't be interested in going with me?

(Lucy *stops, looks at him.*)

Lucy: . . . Are you serious?

Bronco: Yeah. But I warn you. I'm . . . kind of not much of a dancer.

Lucy: (*smiling*) I'll take my chances.

Bronco: . . . So, you'll go with me?

Lucy: I'd love to!

(*They laugh and walk off together arm in arm . . .* FREEZE. . . .)

Point Guard.

You bring the ball down the court.
The pick is set.
The play is set. The movement of
the ball
is faster
than all
the
defensive
hands and heads,
and you
get free.
You pass into the big girl
at the key. She turns
and
shoots and scores.
The crowd roars.

ARNOLD ADOFF

Antaeus

A short story by Borden Deal

In Greek mythology, Antaeus was the son of Gaia (Earth) and Poseidon (Sea). Well known as a giant wrestler, Antaeus was also King of Libya. He would challenge any strangers who passed through his kingdom to wrestle with him. During a match he drew his strength from the earth, and as long as he touched it, he would always win. Gradually he would tire out his opponents and then kill them.

Antaeus was never defeated in his wrestling matches until Hercules, a great adventurer, came along. Hercules noticed that when he lifted Antaeus and set him down again, Antaeus grew ever stronger. So at last Hercules lifted Antaeus high in the air, held him there until he weakened, and then crushed him to death.

This was during the wartime, when lots of people were coming North for jobs in factories and war industries, when people moved around a lot more than they do now, and sometimes kids were thrown into new groups and new lives that were completely different from anything they had ever known before. I remember this one kid, T.J. his name was, from somewhere down South, whose family moved into our building during that time. They'd come North with everything they owned piled into the back seat of an old-model sedan that you wouldn't expect could make the trip, with T.J. and his three younger sisters riding shakily on top of the load of junk.

Our building was just like all the others there, with families crowded into a few rooms, and I guess there were twenty-five or thirty kids about my age in that one building. Of course, there were a few of us who formed a gang and ran together all the time after school, and I was the one who brought T.J. in and started the whole thing.

The building right next door to us was a factory where they made walking dolls. It was a low building with a flat, tarred roof that had a parapet[1] all around it about head-high, and we'd found out a long time before that no one, not even the watchman, paid any attention to the roof because it was higher than any of the other buildings around. So my gang used the roof as a headquarters. We could get up there by crossing over to the fire escape from our own roof on a plank and then going on up. It was a secret place for us, where nobody else could go without our permission.

I remember the day I first took T.J. up there to meet the gang. He was a stocky, robust kid with a shock of white hair, nothing sissy about him except his voice; he talked in this slow, gentle voice like you never heard before. He talked different from any of us and you noticed it right away. But I liked him anyway, so I told him to come on up.

---

1 **parapet:** a low wall or railing

We climbed up over the parapet and dropped down on the roof. The rest of the gang were already there.

"Hi," I said. I jerked my thumb at T.J. "He just moved into the building yesterday."

He just stood there, not scared or anything, just looking, like the first time you see somebody you're not sure you're going to like.

"Hi," Blackie said. "Where are you from?"

"Marion County," T.J. said.

We laughed. "Marion County?" I said. "Where's that?"

He looked at me for a moment like I was a stranger, too. "It's in Alabama," he said, like I ought to know where it was.

"What's your name?" Charley said.

"T.J.," he said, looking back at him. He had pale blue eyes that looked washed-out, but he looked directly at Charley, waiting for his reaction. He'll be all right, I thought. No sissy in him, except that voice. Who ever talked like that?

"T.J.," Blackie said. "That's just initials. What's your real name? Nobody in the world has just initials."

"I do," he said. "And they're T.J. That's all the name I got."

His voice was resolute[2] with the knowledge of his rightness, and for a moment no one had anything to say. T.J. looked around at the rooftop and down at the black tar under his feet. "Down yonder where I come from," he said, "we played out in the woods. Don't you-all have no woods around here?"

"Naw," Blackie said. "There's the park a few blocks over, but it's full of kids and cops and old women. You can't do a thing."

T.J. kept looking at the tar under his feet. "You mean

---

2 **resolute:** determined

you ain't got no fields to raise nothing in?—no watermelons or nothing?"

"Naw," I said scornfully. "What do you want to grow something for? The folks can buy everything they need at the store."

He looked at me again with that strange, unknowing look. "In Marion County," he said, "I had my own acre of cotton and my own acre of corn. It was mine to plant and make ever' year."

He sounded like it was something to be proud of, and in some obscure way it made the rest of us angry. Blackie said, "Who'd want to have their own acre of cotton and corn? That's just work. What can you do with an acre of cotton and corn?"

T.J. looked at him. "Well, you get part of the bale offen your acre," he said seriously. "And I fed my acre of corn to my calf."

We didn't really know what he was talking about, so we were more puzzled than angry; otherwise, I guess, we'd have chased him off the roof and wouldn't let him be part of our gang. But he was strange and different, and we were all attracted by his stolid[3] sense of rightness and belonging, maybe by the strange softness of his voice contrasting our own tones of speech into harshness.

He moved his foot against the black tar. "We could make our own field right here," he said softly, thoughtfully. "Come spring we could raise us what we want to—watermelons and garden truck[4] and no telling what all."

"You'd have to be a good farmer to make these tar roofs grow any watermelons," I said. We all laughed.

But T.J. looked serious. "We could haul us some dirt up here," he said. "And spread it out even and water it,

---

3 **stolid:** showing little or no emotion

4 **garden truck:** vegetables grown for market

and before you know it, we'd have us a crop in here." He looked at us intently. "Wouldn't that be fun?"

"They wouldn't let us," Blackie said quickly.

"I thought you said this was you-all's roof," T.J. said to me. "That you-all could do anything you wanted to up here."

"They've never bothered us," I said. I felt the idea beginning to catch fire in me. It was a big idea, and it took a while for it to sink in; but the more I thought about it, the better I liked it. "Say," I said to the gang. "He might have something there. Just make us a regular roof garden, with flowers and grass and trees and everything. And all ours, too," I said. "We wouldn't let anybody up here except the ones we wanted to."

"It'd take a while to grow trees," T.J. said quickly, but we weren't paying any attention to him. They were all talking about it suddenly, all excited with the idea after I'd put it in a way they could catch hold of it. Only rich people had roof gardens, we knew, and the idea of our own private domain excited them.

"We could bring it up in sacks and boxes," Blackie said. "We'd have to do it while the folks weren't paying any attention to us, for we'd have to come up to the roof of our building and then cross over with it."

"Where could we get the dirt?" somebody said worriedly.

"Out of those vacant lots over close to school," Blackie said. "Nobody'd notice if we scraped it up."

I slapped T.J. on the shoulder. "Man, you had a wonderful idea," I said, and everybody grinned at him, remembering that he had started it. "Our own private roof garden."

He grinned back. "It'll be ourn," he said. "All ourn." Then he looked thoughtful again. "Maybe I can lay my hands on some cotton seed, too. You think we could raise us some cotton?"

We'd started big projects before at one time or another, like any gang of kids, but they'd always petered out for lack of organization and direction. But this one didn't; somehow or other T.J. kept it going all through the winter months. He kept talking about the watermelons and the cotton we'd raise, come spring, and when even that wouldn't work, he'd switch around to my idea of flowers and grass and trees, though he was always honest enough to add that it'd take a while to get any trees started. He always had it on his mind and he'd mention it in school, getting them lined up to carry dirt that afternoon, saying in a casual way that he reckoned a few more weeks ought to see the job through.

Our little area of private earth grew slowly. T.J. was smart enough to start in one corner of the building, heaping up the carried earth two or three feet thick so that we had an immediate result to look at, to contemplate with awe. Some of the evenings T.J. alone was carrying earth up to the building, the rest of the gang distracted by other enterprises or interests, but T.J. kept plugging along on his own, and eventually we'd all come back to him again and then our own little acre would grow more rapidly.

He was careful about the kind of dirt he'd let us carry up there, and more than once he dumped a sandy load over the parapet into the areaway below because it wasn't good enough. He found out the kinds of earth in all the vacant lots for blocks around. He'd pick it up and feel it and smell it, frozen though it was sometimes, and then he'd say it was good growing soil or it wasn't worth anything, and we'd have to go on somewhere else.

Thinking about it now, I don't see how he kept us at it. It was hard work, lugging paper sacks and boxes of dirt all the way up the stairs of our own building, keeping out of the way of the grownups so they wouldn't catch on to what we were doing. They probably wouldn't have cared, for they didn't pay much attention to us, but we wanted to keep it secret anyway. Then we had to go through the trap door to our roof, teeter over a plank to the fire escape, then climb two or three stories to the parapet and drop them down onto the roof. All that for a small pile of earth that sometimes didn't seem worth the effort. But T.J. kept the vision bright within us, his words shrewd and calculated toward the fulfillment of his dream; and he worked harder than any of us. He seemed driven toward a goal that we couldn't see, a particular point in time that would be definitely marked by signs and wonders that only he could see.

The laborious[5] earth just lay there during the cold months, inert and lifeless, the clods lumpy and cold under our feet when we walked over it. But one day it rained, and afterward there was a softness in the air, and the earth was alive and giving again with moisture and warmth.

That evening T.J. smelled the air, his nostrils dilating with the odor of the earth under his feet. "It's spring," he said, and there was a gladness rising in his voice that filled us all with the same feeling. "It's mighty late for it, but it's spring. I'd just about decided it wasn't never gonna get here at all."

We were all sniffing at the air, too, trying to smell it the way that T.J. did, and I can still remember the sweet odor of the earth under our feet. It was the first time in my life that spring and spring earth had meant anything to me. I looked at T.J. then, knowing in a faint way the hunger within him through the toilsome winter months, knowing the dream that lay behind his plan. He was a

---

5 **laborious:** hard-working

new Antaeus, preparing his own bed of strength.

"Planting time," he said. "We'll have to find us some seed."

"What do we do?" Blackie said. "How do we do it?"

"First we'll have to break up the clods," T.J. said. "That won't be hard to do. Then we plant the seeds, and after a while they come up. Then you got you a crop." He frowned. "But you ain't got it raised yet. You got to tend it and hoe it and take care of it, and all the time it's growing and growing, while you're awake and while you're asleep. Then you lay it by when it's growed and let it ripen, and then you got you a crop."

"There's those wholesale seed houses over on Sixth," I said. "We could probably swipe some grass seed over there."

T.J. looked at the earth. "You-all seem mighty set on raising some grass," he said. "I ain't never put no effort into that. I spent all my life trying not to raise grass."

"But it's pretty," Blackie said. "We could play on it and take sunbaths on it. Like having our own lawn. Lots of people got lawns."

"Well," T.J. said. He looked at the rest of us, hesitant for the first time. He kept on looking at us for a moment. "I did have it in mind to raise some corn and vegetables. But we'll plant grass."

He was smart. He knew where to give in. And I don't suppose it made any difference to him, really. He just wanted to grow something, even if it was grass.

"Of course," he said, "I do think we ought to plant a row of watermelons. They'd be mighty nice to eat while we was a-laying on that grass."

We all laughed. "All right," I said. "We'll plant us a row of watermelons."

Things went very quickly then. Perhaps half the roof was covered with the earth, the half that wasn't broken by ventilators, and we swiped pocketfuls of grass seed from the open bins in the wholesale seed house, mingling among the buyers on Saturdays and during the school lunch hour. T.J. showed us how to prepare the earth, breaking up the clods and smoothing it and sowing the grass seed. It looked rich and black now with moisture, receiving of the seed, and it seemed that the grass sprang up overnight, pale green in the early spring.

We couldn't keep from looking at it, unable to believe that we had created this delicate growth. We looked at T.J. with understanding now, knowing the fulfillment of the plan he had carried along within his mind. We had worked without full understanding of the task, but he had known all the time.

We found that we couldn't walk or play on the delicate blades, as we had expected to, but we didn't mind. It was enough just to look at it, to realize that it was the work of our own hands, and each evening the whole gang was there, trying to measure the growth that had been achieved that day.

One time a foot was placed on the plot of ground, one time only, Blackie stepping onto it with sudden bravado.[6] Then he looked at the crushed blades and there was shame in his face. He did not do it again. This was his grass, too, and not to be desecrated.[7] No one said anything, for it was not necessary.

T.J. had reserved a small section for watermelons, and he was still trying to find some seed for it. The wholesale house didn't have any watermelon seeds, and we didn't know where we could lay our hands on them. T.J. shaped the earth into mounds, ready to receive them, three mounds lying in a straight line along the edge of the grass plot.

---

6 **bravado:** pretended courage
7 **desecrated:** treated with disrespect

We had just about decided that we'd have to buy the seeds if we were to get them. It was a violation of our principles, but we were anxious to get the watermelons started. Somewhere or other, T.J. got his hands on a seed catalog and brought it one evening to our roof garden.

"We can order them now," he said, showing us the catalog. "Look!"

We all crowded around, looking at the fat, green watermelons pictured in full color on the pages. Some of them were split open, showing the red, tempting meat, making our mouths water.

"Now we got to scrape up some seed money," T.J. said, looking at us. "I got a quarter. How much you-all got?"

We made up a couple of dollars among us and T.J. nodded his head. "That'll be more than enough. Now we got to decide what kind to get. I think them Kleckley Sweets. What do you-all think?"

He was going into esoteric[8] matters beyond our reach. We hadn't even known there were different kinds of melons. So we just nodded our heads and agreed that yes, we thought the Kleckley Sweets too.

"I'll order them tonight," T.J. said. "We ought to have them in a few days."

"What are you boys doing up here?" an adult voice said behind us.

It startled us, for no one had ever come up here before in all the time we had been using the roof of the factory. We jerked around and saw three men standing near the trap door at the other end of the roof. They weren't policemen or night watchmen, but three men in plump business suits, looking at us. They walked toward us.

---

8 **esoteric:** beyond understanding except to a small group

"What are you boys doing up here?" the one in the middle said again.

We stood still, guilt heavy among us, levied[9] by the tone of voice, and looked at the three strangers.

The men stared at the grass flourishing behind us. "What's this?" the man said. "How did this get up here?"

"Sure is growing good, ain't it?" T.J. said conversationally. "We planted it."

The men kept looking at the grass as if they didn't believe it. It was a thick carpet over the earth now, a patch of deep greenness startling in the sterile industrial surroundings.

"Yes, sir," T.J. said proudly. "We toted that earth up here and planted that grass." He fluttered the seed catalog. "And we're just fixing to plant us some watermelon."

The man looked at him then, his eyes strange and faraway. "What do you mean, putting this on the roof of my building?" he said. "Do you want to go to jail?"

T.J. looked shaken. The rest of us were silent, frightened by the authority of his voice. We had grown up aware of adult authority, of policemen and night watchmen and teachers, and this man sounded like all the others. But it was a new thing to T.J.

"Well, you wasn't using the roof," T.J. said. He paused a moment and added shrewdly, "So we just thought to pretty it up a little bit."

"And sag it so I'd have to rebuild it," the man said sharply. He started turning away, saying to another man beside him, "See that all that junk is shoveled off by tomorrow."

"Yes, sir," the man said.

T.J. started forward. "You can't do that," he said.

---

9 **levied:** forced or imposed

"We toted it up here, and it's our earth. We planted it and raised it and toted it up here."

The man stared at him coldly. "But it's my building," he said. "It's to be shoveled off tomorrow."

"It's our earth," T.J. said desperately. "You ain't got no right!"

The men walked on without listening and descended clumsily through the trapdoor. T.J. stood looking after them, his body tense with anger, until they had disappeared. They wouldn't even argue with him, wouldn't let him defend his earth-rights.

He turned to us. "We won't let 'em do it," he said fiercely. "We'll stay up here all day tomorrow and the day after that, and we won't let 'em do it."

We just looked at him. We knew there was no stopping it.

He saw it in our faces, and his face wavered for a moment before he gripped it into determination. "They ain't got no right," he said. "It's our earth. It's our land. Can't nobody touch a man's own land."

We kept looking at him, listening to the words but knowing that it was no use. The adult world had descended on us even in our richest dream, and we knew there was no calculating the adult world, no fighting it, no winning against it.

We started moving slowly toward the parapet and the fire escape, avoiding a last look at the green beauty of the earth that T.J. had planted for us, had planted deeply in our minds as well as in our experience. We filed slowly over the edge and down the steps to the plank, T.J. coming last, and all of us could feel the weight of his grief behind us.

"Wait a minute," he said suddenly, his voice harsh with the effort of calling.

We stopped and turned, held by the tone of his voice,

and looked up at him standing above us on the fire escape.

"We can't stop them?" he said, looking down at us, his face strange in the dusky light. "There ain't no way to stop 'em?"

"No," Blackie said with finality. "They own the building."

We stood still for a moment, looking up at T.J., caught into inaction by the decision working in his face. He stared back at us, and his face was pale and mean in the poor light, with a bald nakedness in his skin like cripples have sometimes.

"They ain't gonna touch my earth," he said fiercely. "They ain't gonna lay a hand on it! Come on."

He turned around and started up the fire escape again, almost running against the effort of climbing. We followed more slowly, not knowing what he intended. By the time we reached him, he had seized a board and thrust it into the soil, scooping it up and flinging it over the parapet into the areaway below. He straightened and looked at us.

"They can't touch it," he said. "I won't let 'em lay a dirty hand on it!"

We saw it then. He stooped to his labor again and we followed, the gusts of his anger moving in frenzied labor among us as we scattered along the edge of earth, scooping it and throwing it over the parapet, destroying with anger the growth we had nurtured with such tender care. The soil carried so laboriously upward to the light and the sun cascaded swiftly into the dark areaway, the green blades of grass crumpled and twisted in the falling.

It took less time than you would think; the task of destruction is infinitely easier than that of creation. We stopped at the end, leaving only a scattering of loose soil, and when it was finally over, a stillness stood among the group and over the factory building. We looked down at the bare sterility of black tar, felt the harsh texture of it under the soles of our shoes, and the anger had gone out of us, leaving only a sore aching in our minds like overstretched muscles.

T.J. stood for a moment, his breathing slowing from anger and effort, caught into the same contemplation of destruction as all of us. He stooped slowly, finally, and picked up a lonely blade of grass left trampled under our feet and put it between his teeth, tasting it, sucking the greenness out of it into his mouth. Then he started walking toward the fire escape, moving before any of us were ready to move, and disappeared over the edge.

We followed him, but he was already halfway down to the ground, going on past the board where we crossed over, climbing down into the areaway. We saw the last section swing down with his weight, and then he stood on the concrete below us, looking at the small pile of anonymous earth scattered by our throwing. Then he walked across the place where we could see him and disappeared toward the street without glancing back, without looking up to see us watching him.

They did not find him for two weeks.

Then the Nashville police caught him just outside the Nashville freight yards. He was walking along the railroad track, still heading South, still heading home.

As for us, who had no remembered home to call us, none of us ever again climbed the escapeway to the roof.

The Tubeteika Affair

A short story by Vytaute Zilinskaite,
translated by Eve Manning

Dotas charged only a trifle for his advice: one stamp. It could even be a used stamp. Money? Oh no, he wanted none of that. There had been a time when he had charged five kopecks, but his parents had heard about it. So from then on he took only stamps.

The fame of the wise counsellor Dotas in 3B had long ago spread through the school; but after the tubeteika affair was settled, thanks to his ingenuity, it spread far beyond its walls.

But let us go back to the beginning.

Spring had come with a rush. The thin white curtains could not withstand the sun and it poured in through the large windows onto the children. Now, who could be dull or depressed on such a day? There was not a single sombre face, the mood was one of spring gaiety—except for Andrius. He was obviously worried. During break he had hovered around the class wiseacre, evidently with a problem. But Dotas took no notice, played hard to get. So it was only after school was out and they were on their way home that he overtook Dotas in the street and their historic consultation took place.

"Dotas! Wait for me!" Andrius called. "If you can't help me I'm done for!"

The trouble was this. Andrius's father had recently returned from Kirghizia—so far off, that if you went there by train it would take four whole days! But Andrius's father had flown. It was quite different from Lithuania there, he said, all mountains, one after the other, like caravans of camels with grey humps, and snow on top of them. And between the mountains there were valleys with green grass and bright red poppies. But that was not the main thing. Dad had brought back a kind of cap—black, with four corners and embroidered in white silk. It was called a tubeteika—you pronounced it "tyubbytaker." Dad showed it around and then put it in a cupboard, alongside a sombrero—a broad straw hat from Argentina, and a svanka—a white felt cap from the Caucasus. "The start of our family collection of national headdresses," said Dad.

Yesterday, Sunday, Andrius had taken the cap without permission. He wanted to show it off—although actually it was too big for him and kept slipping down over his nose instead of sitting smartly on the back of his head. Well, to make a long story short, he set off in the tubeteika to the bank of the Vilnia. And bent over the water—and the tubeteika slid forward and—

"I ran along the bank and tried to keep up with it. I simply tore along but by the bridge—you know?—the water swirls around, a real whirlpool—and it was gone. Sucked down."

"And they don't know yet at home," said Dotas, half statement, half question.

"Would I be picking your brains if they knew?" sobbed Andrius, then, remembering, felt in his pocket and pulled out a stamp with a zebra and a chocolate in silver paper. The stamp was crumpled and the sweet had been flattened from long existence in his pocket. He held out his gifts to Dotas.

Dotas examined the stamp and then returned it.

"Defective—a reject."

"I didn't know," mumbled a confused Andrius. "I'll get you another. A whole series, with spiders!"

Dotas nodded staidly and relapsed into concentrated thought, chewing the chocolate. Promising folds appeared on his forehead.

"Listen, then. Ask your father what is the capital of Kirghizia. Secondly, how many schools there are. Only do it so that he doesn't suspect anything. That's all," he said at last.

"That's all?" repeated Andrius, disappointed.

"For the present—all. The rest comes later," said Dotas with a sly look. "Find out, and tell me." He turned on his heel and ran off home.

Just before going to bed that evening Andrius tackled his father, approaching in roundabout ways.

"Dad, what's the capital of Portugal?"

"Lisbon."

"Lisbon? And Estonia?"

"You ought to know that! Tallinn."

"Oh, of course—I'd forgotten. And Kirghizia?"

"Kirghizia? Frunze."

"Frunze, Frunze, Frunze," he whispered to fix it in his mind. "And Dad! How many schools would there be in Frunze?"

"A good many, for certain."

"As many as thirty?"

"I expect so. They have a lot of children there."

"Thirty schools. And the forms—I suppose they have them like ours—three A, three B, and so on all through the school."

"Of course. A and B and maybe C, D and E. I told you there are a lot of children."

"Smashing!"

"I'm glad to see you taking an interest in distant parts," said Dad approvingly. "You can always ask me if there's anything you want to know, I'll be glad to tell you."

"Not less than thirty," Dotas repeated thoughtfully after he had heard Andrius's report during the first break. He did not hurry with his advice, and indeed, it seemed doubtful whether he had any to give because he suddenly asked, "What's your number in the form book?"

"Fifteen."

"Fifteen—that's better, in fact it's good," he mumbled. "Now, this is what you must do. Write to Frunze. To a pupil who is number fifteen in form 3B."

"But what shall I write?"

"Send some kind of souvenir—a postcard or a badge or something, and ask for a tubeteika."

"So that's it!"

So clever and yet so simple! Couldn't be simpler. Why couldn't he have thought of that himself? Obviously he felt disgusted with himself.

Dotas looked at him, narrow-eyed, and he suddenly wondered uneasily whether the wiseacre could read his thoughts and perhaps take offense.

"What a grand idea!" he flattered his counselor.

"Don't write only one letter," said the latter weightily. "Nothing might come of it. Write to all the thirty schools, address the letters school number one, two and so on, Frunze, Kirghizia. Pupil number fifteen in form three B—the three A and C too, all the threes."

"How many letters will that be? Surely I don't need so many."

"Better be safe. Let's see—four forms each in thirty schools—h'm! A hundred and twenty. Well, that makes it a sure thing, one of the hundred and twenty will certainly send it."

"Well—thanks awfully!"

"That's all right. If they send two, then one for me?"

"Of course!"

Then the work began. Andrius cut the pages of ten notebooks into neat sheets, emptied his collection of badges and pulled all the unused stamps out of his album. A hundred and twenty letters—that was no joke, he had not written so many in his whole life.

> Dear unknown friend,
>
> I do not yet know your name, but like me you are number fifteen in the form book and for that reason I am writing to you. I have had a piece of very bad luck. My dad was in Kirghizia and brought back a souvenir. A black tubeteika with white embroidery. And I accidentally dropped it in the river. Dad does not know yet but when he does there'll be bad trouble. Please save me, send me a tubeteika, and then let's go on corresponding. I am enclosing a souvenir, a badge from my city Vilnius. Write to me at school so that they do not know at home. That's all.
>
> All the best,
>
> Andrius

"That's all right," said Dotas when Andrius showed him the letter and then asked him to add, "Dotas, a representative of Lithuanian youth, sends you greetings and would be very glad to make your acquaintance."

Andrius sighed but wrote it. A hundred and twenty times.

A week passed and then a second. Dad went away on another trip without discovering the loss of the tubeteika. Andrius lived in a torment of suspense until at last, one day in May, the teacher suddenly said, "Andrius, there's a parcel for you in the teacher's room, go and fetch it."

Andrius went with beating heart. A package wrapped in pink paper lay on the long table. Andrius picked it up, went out into the passage, then with trembling hands tore off the paper and pulled out—a tubeteika!—exactly like the one Dad had brought, black, four-cornered and embroidered with white silk. Marvelous! And there was a letter, too.

> Dear Andrius,
>
> I was very pleased to get your letter. Thank you for the badge. I bought a tubeteika at once and am glad to give it to you. I have wanted for a long time to have a pen-friend in another republic. My mother says that there are no mountains in Lithuania and that you do not drink koumiss, that is mare's milk. A pity because koumiss is very good, I love it. I collect butterflies, I have a lot. If you can, please catch a Lithuanian butterfly for me. Write me more about yourself and your friends and your school and your republic. And I will write, too. Greetings to your youth representative Dotas,
>
> All the best,
>
> Asan

Returning to the classroom, Andrius met Dotas's eyes. He wore a proudly triumphant look. They exchanged winks.

The next day again the teacher announced a parcel for Andrius.

Again Andrius stood before the long table—but this time he saw four packages. He did not even wait to open them—the contents were obvious; he scooped them up and scuttled back to the classroom. One tubeteika he would give the wiseacre as agreed, one for himself, but the third and fourth and fifth—? Oh, something would turn up.

After school Dotas tried on the tubeteika in the cloakroom.

"A bit big, but it'll do."

You might at least have said thank you, thought Andrius.

When the teacher summoned Andrius the next day she sounded puzzled.

Andrius went reluctantly, very unhappy, his legs like rubber. And with reason. The whole table was piled with almost identical packages. A mountain of them! Fifty at least, maybe more. How on earth would he carry them all? And what was he to do with them? In his confusion it took him a long time to gather them up. And it was all the fault of that clever donkey Dotas.

Andrius carried the packages to the cloakroom, rolled them in his raincoat and tied the sleeves. When he returned to the classroom he did not even look at Dotas; but after school he grabbed the bundle and ran to overtake him, to give them all to him and let him do what he liked with them since he was so clever. However, Dotas heard panting behind him, turned, saw Andrius crimson with fury, and ran for his life.

"Stop!" howled Andrius. "Stop! These are yours! You hear me? Yours! You told me to write all those letters! Take them or I'll tell the teacher!"

But Dotas pelted off without turning.

When he got home Andrius dived into the cellar, found a clean sack, tipped all the packages into it, pushed it into a corner and covered it with all sorts of old rubbish. Later, he could get it out, read the letters and seek advice from his own wits, how on earth to get out of this new snarl he was in.

At school he kept very quiet. He did not want to be noticed. He never looked at Dotas.

At break the headmaster himself sought him out.

"I think you'd better explain the meaning of all this. Otherwise I'll have to send for your parents."

The pile of packages on the table in the teachers' room was as big as ever. Andrius looked at it, horrified.

"I—I'll explain—later," he whispered and rather surprisingly the headmaster left it at that.

It certainly was a case of out of the frying-pan. Andrius again collected the armful of packages, took them to the cloakroom and bundled them into his coat. Dotas had prudently disappeared without waiting for the last lesson.

The sack in the cellar was almost full and nearly too heavy to lift.

Later on he discovered a package he had pushed into his pocket and forgotten. He unwrapped it and saw a tubeteika—*such* a tubeteika, velvet, and embroidered with blue silk, and it fitted him perfectly, too. And a letter.

> Dear distant Andrius,
>
> What an unusual name but a nice one. The whole form envied me being the fifteenth and getting a letter from Lithuania. I was dreadfully upset about your needing a tubeteika so badly because I have not any money to buy one and send it at once. And I cannot ask mum. Dad was killed in a motor accident and I have nine brothers and sisters, three older than I am and the rest younger, so it is difficult for mum with all of us. But I asked auntie for velvet and silk and my sisters and friends have helped me. They all send you greetings. Do you like our tubeteika? I am so glad to give it to you, Andrius. My granddad and grandma live on the bank of a great big lake called Issyk-Kul.

> It is beautiful there. Come and see it when you grow up. I must stop now but I shall be waiting for your reply. I would like to have you for a pen-friend.
>
> Wishing you all the very best,
>
> Aigyul

Reading the letter Andrius felt himself blush for shame. He remembered it in the night and cried. He cried for a long time, and in the morning his whole face was swollen.

That day there were only three packages on the table. The flood was dwindling. The day after there was only a letter.

> "Dear Andrius," wrote a boy called Tologen, "I am sorry I cannot send you a tubeteika, I feel very bad about it but it is not my fault. I have been to all the shops where they have always had tubeteikas but now there was not one, they told me they had had plenty but they were all sold out. Actually, it is girls who wear tubeteikas here, boys wear a kind of felt hat with two little peaks. It is call ak-kalpak and it is boat-shaped. But please do not worry, as soon as any appear I will send you a tubeteika. I would like to have you for a pen-friend. I am enclosing a picture postcard of the Ala-Tau Mountains. And please do send me pictures of Lithuania, especially the sea. I have never seen the sea but on the map Lithuania is right by it. Honestly, I tried to get you the tubeteika."

Andrius read this letter in the classroom during break and he had hardly finished when the monitor came and said the headmaster wanted him and added that the form mistress was already in his office.

To say Andrius was uncomfortable would be putting it mildly. He stared at his boots and his ears burned. And then—suddenly—he decided to make a clean breast of it all.

"But why did you send a hundred and twenty letters?" asked the headmaster. "Wouldn't one have been enough?"

"It was Dotas who advised me to." Andrius was no tell-tale, but since Dotas was avoiding him, then let people know the sort of adviser he was. "I wanted to write one but he said it must be a hundred and twenty. It took me three days, my hands were sore, and then he made me add a greeting from him."

Now Dotas will get it, thought Andrius vengefully. Serve him right!

But the teacher only laughed. "You don't have to follow every bit of advice that's given. Use your own head! You're a head taller than he is and you get better marks, too!"

His eyes went down to his boots again. He was crimson with shame. It was true, he ought to have done his own thinking. He wasn't a bit of a kid. He would soon be in the fourth form.

At the end of the last lesson the teacher gave Dotas a meaning look.

"Well, wise adviser, what has your wisdom to offer now? You know what I'm talking about?"

"I know," said Dotas without any great sign of confusion.

"And what's your advice now?"

Dotas stared out of the window. It gave a view of the railway and a train with small green coaches, looking like toys in the distance. A fold appeared on the forehead of the sage.

Everybody knew the whole story by this time and all eyes were fixed on Dotas. How would he wriggle out of this one?

"My advice is," said Dotas with dignity, "to distribute the tubeteikas and letters to all those who'd like to have pen-friends in Kirghizia. There!"

"Good for you!" said the teacher.

The form literally howled with delight and Andrius felt as though he had been sandbagged. Idiot—such a simple solution! Couldn't be simpler! Hand around the tubeteikas and let the kids answer the letters and have pen-friends and exchange souvenirs. Why hadn't he thought of it himself? Of course, he might have, but Dotas had thought of it first. It wasn't for nothing the kids said he'd a head on him!

It wasn't worth bearing a grudge against Dotas. There was too much to be done. He dragged the sack into the classroom and it wasn't only his pals from 3B who wanted to correspond with children in Kirghizia. A and C too were clamoring for letters. Andrius kept Asan and Aigyul for himself, however. They would be his own friends.

Now the whole form dreams of visiting the Ala-Tau Mountains and Lake Issyk-Kul. They probably will, too, if not this summer, then the next. Dotas advises it, too.

Running Lava Falls

From the non-fiction book
Women in the Wilderness by China Galland

The tension this morning is like a wired fence sparking at the slightest touch. Today we run Lava Falls. Water flow is about fifteen hundred cubic feet per second, giving Lava a solid ten rating on the scale of difficulty for rapids. Number ten. Lava marks the outer limit.

Our plan for running it is to set ourselves up for the "slot," a narrow section of water that shoots straight through the falls and gives us our only chance of avoiding major obstacles. The slot is only three feet in the midst of a churning hundred-foot-wide expanse of falling water. We have only seconds to make our move; a foot off on either side in that fast current means that we miss and all hell breaks loose.

Only six of us will paddle through Lava. Barb Dupuis, our paddleboat captain, thinks the only fair way to select our crew is to draw straws. We settle for twigs, breaking six off short as a sign of being a crew member. At least ten of us want to paddle. Though our chances of flipping the boat are high—fifty-fifty—my preference is to paddle, knowing that at least I'll be thrown clean, no "death lines" or gear to get tangled in, to trap me in a rapid underneath a capsized boat.

"Death lines" are loose long ends of the webbing used to tie the boat loads down. If a boat flips and a piece of webbing wraps around you underneath the boat it can easily become a "death line." When we tie the loads down this morning, we help with all possibilities in mind, checking carefully to see that all gear is secured and no webbing is left loose. The mist that covers much of our day-to-day life is burned off in the heat of the apparent risks we are taking. The possibility of death is no longer veiled or mere morbid consideration; it is valid and essential to take into account.

If we make the slot, Barb will yell the command "Drop!" as we go into the first enormous wave. Then we'll automatically pop back up, released from the pressure of thousands of gallons of water pouring over us, and paddle like fury until the rapid ends. We agree and quietly position ourselves in the raft.

We pull out into the current, back paddling to position ourselves before being swept over the falls. Though my heart is pounding, my breath is steady. We are poised, ready to spring. We drift closer. From the back of the raft where she is standing, directing our strokes, Barb yells "Drop!" and we hit the floor, keeping the weight low and central. I'm in the back next to Barb to help rudder as we make our dive. The front of the raft comes up and a solid wall of gray water comes pouring down on us from overhead. It feels as if we're capsizing end over end. I can't tell if I'm in the boat or out of it, and then in a split second I know that I'm out as the next twenty-five-foot wave engulfs me, plunging me beneath the surface.

I begin to panic but realize that I'm only wasting time. All there is to do is breathe whenever possible and relax in the middle of this intense turbulence. Nothing more. Nothing less. Time balloons, full and swollen; seconds expand into minutes; there is only the gray thundering water, the constant boiling, and my presence of mind. I look over my right shoulder and see an immense wave that will take me under again. I take a deep breath and give over to the forces of a wild river, an explosion of water. Twenty-five feet over my head, the wave tip curls, breaks, and crashes down on me, pummeling me into the vortex of the turbulence itself. Down, around, until the next moment, tossed up like a twig to the surface again. I am through the rapid. It has all happened within forty-five seconds.

I look around and see that the paddle boat has not capsized and is just upstream of me, midriver, close enough for me to swim to. Somehow I still have my paddle in my hand. Someone grabs it, pulling me to the boat, then grabs me by the seat of my pants, frantically catapulting me back into the raft. I'm safe. So is Barb, who washed out with me. They have pulled her back in just before me. We give a shout. We're all accounted for and the boat has not flipped.

Barb quickly assumes command again and orders us to bail with a frenzy. The boat is filled to the brim with water and is barely maneuverable. We have to pull into an eddy and empty it so that we aren't swept into the next rapid downstream uncontrolled. More important, we are the rescue boat for the last snout rig, which is just beginning to make its run. By the time we're able to pull into the eddy, they've made a beautiful run and have no need of us. We can relax. We pull to shore and turn the boat over, emptying hundreds of gallons of water back into the river.

I am left stripped, vulnerable, and bare. I feel transparent, like a child, unable to disguise my feelings. The pounding of my heart vibrates throughout my entire body. I am safe, there are friends holding me, laughing. I shake my head as though waking from a dream and let out a loud "whoopeeee!"

Disciplines

I had been working two days
Laying up this stone wall for
Them, walking home to eat a
Sandwich, when they invited
Me inside to share their dinner.
Sat with the father and two sons.
His wife had spread out the
Plastic tablecloth and it was
On that we ate macaroni,
Folded white bread, stirred
Tang into spring water. I was
The only one to use a napkin,
The only one to wash my hands
Before sitting down to eat, and
When we went back to work
The only one to use my
Hands laying the rock. One
Climbed up into the backhoe,
The other drove the pickup,
And the youngest son came up
To me, thin as a rake handle,
Hair in his eyes and bored asked,
"What d'yah want me to do?"

BOB ARNOLD

The Paper-Boy

In the first morning light
the paper-boy threw
the news of the world
Against closed doors.
The early light accompanied him
Like a silent, obedient dog
But he did not see it, he was
  working
Distributing world.
Only after the last bundle
Made up of the waste of yesterday
was thrown away with a
  practised but indifferent hand,
Did he become aware of his loyal
  companion.
Whistling, the boy rode his cycle
  home.
The morning ran alongside,
A golden, barking dog.

Walter Bauer
translated by Henry Beissel

Perspective

my mother in the hayrack
pitching the hay up
into the black box of the loft
where my father's pitchfork took it,
tossed it to the back;
a synchronism asserting itself
through the dry slither of hay,
the pivot of her fork, his fork,
the fulcrum of arm and necessity

until my father's voice—never hers—
saying, *time for a rest*,
and why should I still need to know
if it was because he tired first
or if it was not her right to choose?
And tugging up lately in myself,
like fresh forksful of hay,
a third possibility,
that she refused to give in first,
and a fourth,
that he knew this
and stopped for her sake—
unnerving me
with the increasing complexities
of their lives.

LEONA GOM

From Behind The Red Line

From the book by Tod Hartje
with Lawrence Martin

Following his graduation from Harvard, Tod Hartje was drafted to play hockey with the Winnipeg Jets. However, the managers of the team thought he needed further training before he actually joined the Jets. So they sent him to Russia, where he became the first North American to play for a professional Soviet hockey team. In this selection from his book From Behind the Red Line, *Hartje describes playing his first game with his team, Sokol Kiev, against the Soviet Wings.*

Game days were quiet. A short practice in the morning was followed by a lunch with a special treat—a big heap of black caviar, a Soviet luxury that I got quickly hooked on. Then we napped, had a team meeting, and went for the game-day walk—about half an hour around the camp grounds. Next came the obligatory tea and sweets. The Soviet players downed huge hunks of thick chocolate, which according to the team malnutritionist would provide energy through game time. Such a theory was prevalent in the West, but later studies had shown that the boost from sweets only lasted about an hour and was followed by a crash. I took it easy on the chocolate and at the rink before the game avoided the thick black coffee that the Soviet players also relished.

I received my uniform. My white jersey was so big it could have fit over a tank. I asked for a smaller size but was told that everyone got extra, extra, extra large. Mine came down to just below the knees. The material was so heavy it felt like chain mail. . . .

Luckily I had my own sticks, shin pads, and other gear. As with the jerseys, everyone on the team was given the same oversize pads and oversize hockey gloves and oversize sticks. The dressing room turned carpentry shop as players sawed pads and gloves, trying to get them to fit their bodies. Like the farm team, they hung great gobs of smelly laundry in the room, and, not having modern blowtorches, employed burning newspapers to generate the heat that could curve their sticks. . . .

The players were allotted three Russian-made sticks each and these were expected to last several games. They looked with considerable envy at my imported ones, more because of the label, which meant status, than the difference in quality.

While I was getting emotionally psyched up for the game, my teammates throughout the day maintained a downcast demeanor, as if they were preparing for a trip to the dentist. With one or two exceptions the emotional level was remarkably even-keeled. It was what the philosophy of the Soviet collective demanded and what hockey genius Papa Tarasov had taught. No individual was to stand apart from the others. In the 1970s, the outstanding player of his era, fireball forward Valery Kharlamov, was once denounced by Tarasov for blaming a teammate for not being in position. The puck carrier, Tarasov admonished Kharlamov, is the servant of the other players, not vice versa.

Somewhat paradoxically, while not emphasizing individuality, the Russians stressed initiative and offense. I'd read another Tarasov dictum on Soviet sport. "It is not possible to play a defensive game against a strong team and win, except perhaps once, by sheer luck. Because when you play a defensive game, you forfeit the main thing—initiative. And it is initiative that most often decides who will win."

Before the Wings game the dressing room was solemn. We had seen no film of the team we would oppose and there was no discussion of any special tactics to be employed. Captain Sherayev, as he had done for the exhibition games, gave just one exhortation. As we were getting up to go out on the ice, he shouted, "Daveye! Daveye! Daveye!" "Let's go! Let's go! Let's go!"

Skating around in the warm-up I occasionally glanced to the stands to catch spectators eyeing me and finger-pointing. There'd been considerable local press on my presence prior to the season opener, prompting me to think that their main reason for agreeing to having me here was as a promotional plus to attract fans to the games.

They put me on left wing on the fourth line. To the annoyance of many in the crowd I was benched for the entire first period. "Amerikanski! Amerikanski!" they chanted. Heading into the locker room at intermission, Bogdanov told me to get ready to play. "I've been getting ready two and half months," I felt like telling him.

The fever was rising, though, and when I stepped on the ice I was anything but an example of an even-keeled collectivist. I was as psyched as I had been in Boston, and within seconds whipped off a shot that almost snagged the corner. The fans were instantly behind me, cheering each time I touched the puck. "Daveye! Daveye! Daveye!"

After my near goal, I set one up but my linemate missed a clear shot. I belted one Wings player with a hit that made everyone take note, and it was only natural that I got sent off to the penalty box in my first period of action in Soviet hockey. It was for an innocent pull on the hip of an opponent with the end of my stick—something that happens a hundred times a game in the NHL without a call.

In the third period, score tied 3–3, we had a face-off in the Wings' zone. The puck went back to our defenseman and instinctively I headed for the goal. We call it crashing the net, and it's common to our game. But it's something that the Soviets don't do. They will fan out in a situation like that, looking to get open for some fancy passing. They don't realize that crashing the goal gives you an excellent chance to deflect in the shot or pick up a rebound.

As I headed in, the defenseman wound up and fired. I powered through someone and was just three or four feet in front of the goal when I felt the puck. It glanced off my hip and zipped into the net without the goal-tender even budging. I was shocked, and hesitated momentarily, wanting to make sure they would count it.

When they did, when the light went on, I double-pumped, the crowd went crazy, and I collected the puck as a souvenir.

Goal! Tod Daleovich Hartje! Teammates whacked me on the helmet; Bogdanov slapped me on the shoulder; the doc grabbed me by the arms and shook; a spectator ran to me at the bench with flowers and the Soviet fans cheered. They cheered like I was one of their own.

No Man Is an Island

From the essay "Meditation 17"
by John Donne

No man is an island, entire of itself; every man is a piece of the continent, a part of the main.[1] If a clod be washed away by the sea, Europe is the less, as well as if a promontory[2] were, as well as if a manor of thy friend's or of thine own were. Any man's death diminishes me because I am involved in mankind, and therefore never send to know for whom the bell tolls; it tolls for thee.

1 **main:** mainland
2 **promontory:** a peak of land that juts out into a body of water

I Am a Rock

A winter's day
In a deep and dark December;
I am alone,
Gazing from my window
To the streets below
On a freshly fallen silent shroud of snow.
I am a rock, I am an island.

I've built walls,
A fortress deep and mighty,
That none may penetrate.
I have no need of friendship;
Friendship causes pain.
It's laughter and it's loving I disdain.
I am a rock, I am an island.

Don't talk of love;
But I've heard the word before;
It's sleeping in my memory,
I won't disturb the slumber
Of feelings that have died.
If I never loved
I never would have cried.
I am a rock, I am an island.

I have my books
And my poetry to protect me;
I am shielded in my armour,
Hiding in my room,
Safe within my womb.
I touch no one and no one touches me.
I am a rock, I am an island.

And a rock feels no pain;
And an island never cries.

PAUL SIMON

The Friends of KWAN MING

A short story by Paul Yee

When his father died, the peasant Kwan Ming was forced to sell his little plot of paddy and the old family house to pay for the burial. After the funeral, Kwan Ming looked around at the banana trees surrounding his village, and saw that he had nothing left to his name—not even one chipped roof tile. He had just enough money to buy a steamship ticket to the New World, where he had heard jobs were plentiful.

"I can start a new life there," he told his mother. "I will send money home."

The voyage lasted six weeks, over rocky waves and through screaming storms. Kwan Ming huddled together with hundreds of other Chinese deep in the ship's hold. There he became fast friends with Chew Lap, Tam Yim and Wong Foon—men from neighboring villages. If one friend took sick, the others fetched him food and water. If one friend had bad luck gambling, the others lent him money to recover his losses. Together the three men ate, told jokes, and shared their dreams for the future.

When they arrived in the New World, everyone scattered throughout the port city to search for work. Kwan Ming hurried to the warehouse district, to the train station, and to the waterfront, but doors slammed in his face because he was Chinese. So he went to every store and laundry in Chinatown, and to every farm outside town. But there was not a job to be found anywhere, for there were too many men looking for work in a country that was still too young.

Every night Kwan Ming trudged back to the inn where he was staying with his three friends. Like him, they, too, had been searching for work but had found nothing. Every night, as they ate their meager meal of rice dotted with soya sauce, the friends shared information about the places they had visited and the people they had met. And every night Kwan Ming worried more and more about his mother, and how she was faring.

"If I don't find work soon, I'm going back to China," Chew Lap declared one evening.

"What for, fool?" asked Tam Yim. "Things are worse there!"

"But at least I will be with my family!" retorted Chew Lap.

"Your family needs money for food more than they need your company," Wong Foon commented. "Don't forget that."

Then a knock was heard at the door, and the innkeeper pushed his way into the tiny attic room.

"Good news!" he cried out. "I have found a job for each of you!"

The men leapt eagerly to their feet.

"Three of the jobs are well-paying and decent,"

announced the innkeeper. "But the fourth job is, well . . ." He coughed sadly.

For the first time since they had met, the four men eyed one another warily, like four hungry cats about to pounce on a bird.

"The biggest bakery in Chinatown needs a worker," said the innkeeper. "You'll always be warm next to the oven. Who will go?"

"You go, Chew Lap," Kwan Ming said firmly. "Your parents are ill and need money for medicine."

"The finest tailor in Chinatown wants an apprentice," continued the innkeeper. "The man who takes this job will be able to throw away those thin rags you wear."

"That's for you, Tam Yim," declared Kwan Ming. "You have four little ones waiting for food in China."

"The best shoemaker in Chinatown needs an assistant," said the innkeeper. "He pays good wages. Who wants to cut leather and stitch boots?"

"You go, Wong Foon," Kwan Ming stated. "You said the roof of your house in China needs repair. Better get new tiles before the rainy season starts."

"The last job is for a houseboy." The innkeeper shook his head. "The pay is low. The boss owns the biggest mansion in town, but he is also the stingiest man around!"

Kwan Ming had no choice but to take this job, for he knew his mother would be desperate for money. So off he went.

The boss was fatter than a cast-iron stove and as cruel as a blizzard at midnight. Kwan Ming's room was next to the furnace, so black soot and coal dust covered his pillow and blankets. It was difficult to save money, and the servants had to fight over the leftovers for their meals.

Every day Kwan Ming swept and washed every floor in the mansion. He moved the heavy oak tables and rolled up the carpets. The house was so big, that when Kwan Ming finally finished cleaning the last room, the first one was dirty all over again.

One afternoon Kwan Ming was mopping the front porch when his boss came running out. In his hurry, he slipped and crashed down the stairs. Kwan Ming ran over to help, but the fat man turned on him.

"You turtle!" he screamed as his neck purpled and swelled. "You lazy oaf! You doorknob! You rock-brain! You're fired!"

Kwan Ming stood silently for a long moment. Then he spoke. "Please, sir, give me another chance. I will work even harder if you let me stay."

The boss listened and his eyes narrowed. Then he coughed loudly. "Very well, Kwan Ming, I won't fire you," he said. "But I will have to punish you, for you have ruined this suit and scuffed my boots and made me miss my dinner."

Kwan Ming nodded miserably.

"Then find me the following things in three days' time!" the boss ordered. "Bring me a fine woolen suit that will never tear. Bring me a pair of leather boots that will never wear out. And bring me forty loaves of bread that will never go stale. Otherwise you are finished here, and I will see that you never find another job!"

Kwan Ming shuddered as he ran off. The old man's demands sounded impossible. Where would he find such items?

In despair, Kwan Ming wandered through the crowded streets of Chinatown. He sat on the raised wooden sidewalk because he had nowhere else to go.

Suddenly, familiar voices surrounded him.

"Kwan Ming, where have you been?"

"Kwan Ming, how is your job?"

"Kwan Ming, why do you never visit us?"

Kwan Ming looked up and saw his three friends smiling down at him. They pulled him up and pulled him off to the teahouse, where they ate and drank. When Kwan Ming told his friends about his predicament, the men clapped him on the shoulder.

"Don't worry!" exclaimed Tam Yim. "I'll make the woolen suit you need."

"I'll make the boots," added Wong Foon.

"And I'll make the bread," exclaimed Chew Lap.

Three days later, Kwan Ming's friends delivered the goods they had promised. An elegant suit of wool hung over a gleaming pair of leather boots, and forty loaves of fresh-baked bread were lined up in neat rows on the dining-room table.

Kwan Ming's boss waddled into the room and his eyes lit up. He put on the suit, and his eyebrows arched in surprise at how well it fit. Then he sat down and tried on the boots, which slid onto his feet as if they had been buttered.

Then the boss sliced into the bread and started eating. The bread was so soft, so sweet, and so moist that he couldn't stop. Faster and faster he chewed. He ate twelve loaves, then thirteen, then twenty.

The boss's stomach swelled like a circus tent, and his feet bloated out like balloons. But the well-sewn suit and sturdy boots held him tight like a gigantic sausage. The man shouted for help. He tried to stand up, but he couldn't even get out of his chair. He kicked his feet about like a baby throwing a tantrum.

But before anyone could do a thing, there was a shattering *Bang!*

Kwan Ming stared at the chair and blinked his eyes in astonishment. For there was nothing left of his boss.

He had exploded into a million little pieces.

LECTURE

"You can't because you are a boy"
Are words that really do annoy me.
And my toes with sorrow curl
At "Don't do that dear, you're a girl."

If you want to be a sailor
Learn to sail dear.
If you want to be a teacher
Try to teach.
And when you're older
It may be
That you will teach or go to sea
Or drive a truck
Or build a barn
Or weave a carpet out of yarn
Or be a doctor to a cat
And I will say
"I knew you could
Because you're you
And awfully good
At what you do
And that is that."

KARLA KUSKIN

The Friday Everything Changed

A short story by Anne Hart

The last hour of school on Friday afternoons was for Junior Red Cross. The little kids would get out their Junior Red Cross pins and put them on and us big kids would start elbowing down the aisles to the book cupboard at the back to see who would get the interesting magazines. There was a big pile of them and they were of two kinds: the *National Geographic* and the *Junior Red Cross News*. Because the boys were stronger and sat near the back they usually got the *National Geographics* first, which meant they could spend the rest of Red Cross looking at African ladies wearing nothing on top, while us girls had to be satisfied with the *Junior Red Cross News,* which showed little African kids wearing lots of clothes and learning how to read. Apart from the magazines for the big kids and maybe the teacher reading a story to the little kids, about the only thing that happened regularly during Red Cross was picking the two boys who would carry water the next week.

In our school the water bucket always stood on a shelf at the front of the room just behind the teacher's desk. First you'd make a paper cup out of a piece of scribbler paper, then you'd grab the teacher's attention from wherever it happened to be and then up you'd go to the front of the room for a drink from the water bucket.

It was kind of interesting to stand at the front of the room behind the teacher's desk and drink water. The school looked different from up there and sometimes you could get just a glimpse of an idea of what the teacher thought she was all about. I mean, from the front, looking down on those rows of kids with their heads bent over their desks and the sun coming in the windows and the blackboards and all that stuff on the walls, you might almost think, at first glance, that you were looking at one of those real city schools—like in the health books—where the kids were all so neat and all the same size. But after the first strange moment it just became our school again, because you had to start adding in things like the coal stove and the scarred old double desks and the kids themselves. I mean, we just didn't look like the kids in those pictures. Maybe it was because we were so many different sizes—from the kids snuffling in the front rows over their Nan and Dan readers to the big boys hunched over their desks at the back—maybe it was because we wore so many heavy clothes all the time, or maybe it was because of something that wasn't even there at all but seemed to be on the faces of the kids in those city pictures: a look as if they liked being where they were.

But all that's a long way from Junior Red Cross and who would carry the water.

The water for our school came from a pump at the

railway station, which was about a quarter of a mile away. One day long ago a health inspector had come around and had announced that water must be made available to the school. For a while there had been some talk of digging a well but in the end we got a big, shiny, galvanized water bucket and permission to use the railway station pump. And from that day on—for all the boys—the most important thing that happened at school, even more important than softball, was who would get to carry the water.

If you were a boy it was something you started dreaming about in Grade 1, even though there was not the remotest chance it could ever happen to you before at least Grade 5, and only then if the teacher thought you were big and strong enough. You dreamed about it partly because carrying the water meant you were one of the big guys, and carrying the water meant you could get away from school for maybe half an hour at a time. But mostly you dreamed about it because carrying the water was something real, and had absolutely nothing whatever to do with Nan and Dan and all that stuff.

So every Friday afternoon toward the end of Red Cross, when it got to be time for the teacher to pick the two boys who would go for water the next week, all the *National Geographics* came to rest like huge butterflies folding up their yellow wings and a big hush fell all over the back rows. And that's the way it had always been until one extraordinary afternoon when, right out of the blue, just after the teacher had picked Ernie Chapman and Garnet Dixon to carry the water, my seatmate, Alma Niles, put up her hand and said: "Why can't girls go for the water, too?"

If one of those German planes, like in the war movies, had suddenly appeared over the school and dropped a bomb, we all couldn't have been more surprised. A silence fell over the room and in that silence everyone looked at the teacher.

Now our teacher that year was named Miss Ralston and even though she came from River Hibbert we all liked her quite a lot. She was strict but she was never really mean like some of the teachers we'd had. Because she was young (she'd just finished Grade 11 the year before herself—River Hibbert had fancy things like Grade 11) she'd had quite a rough time the first week of school with the bigger boys. But she was pretty big herself and after she'd strapped most of them up at the front of the room before our very eyes (and even the little kids could see that it really hurt) things had settled down. The boys kind of admired Miss Ralston for strapping so hard, and us girls admired her because she was so pretty and wore nylon stockings and loafers all the time. But the really unusual thing about Miss Ralston was the way she sometimes stopped in the middle of a lesson and looked at us as if we were real people, instead of just a lot of kids who had to be pushed through to their next grades. And that was why, on that Friday afternoon when Alma Niles put up her hand and said: "Why can't girls go for the water, too?" we all turned and looked at Miss Ralston first instead of just bursting out laughing at Alma right away.

And Miss Ralston, instead of saying, "Whoever heard of girls going for the water?" or, "Are you trying to be saucy, Alma?" like any other teacher would, said nothing at all for a moment but just looked very hard at Alma, who had gone quite white with the shock of dropping such a bombshell. After a long moment, when she finally spoke, Miss Ralston, instead of saying, "Why that's out of the question, Alma," threw a bombshell of her own: "I'll think about that," she said—as if, you know, she *would*—"and I'll let you know next Friday."

The trouble started right away as soon as we got into the schoolyard, because all the boys knew, from the moment Miss Ralston had spoken, that something of theirs was being threatened and that, as long as there was the remotest chance that any girl might get to carry the water, they had to do everything in their power to stop it. Like driving a tractor or playing hockey for the Toronto Maple Leafs, carrying water was real, and because it was real it belonged to them.

So they went right for Alma as soon as she came out of school and that was when another funny thing happened. Instead of just standing back and watching Alma get beaten up, as we usually did when the boys were after someone, the girls rushed right in to try and help her. In the first place we all liked Alma, and in the second place we all had seen, as clearly as the boys, what our carrying the water might mean; that, incredibly, we, too, might get to skip school for half an hour at a time, that we, too, might get to sneak into Rowsell's store on the way back and, most dizzying thought of all, that we too might get to do something real.

And, because we were so intoxicated by the whole idea, and took the boys so much by surprise by standing up to them, we somehow managed to get Alma and ourselves out of the schoolyard with only a few bruises and torn stockings, leaving the boys in possession of the schoolyard where, as we could glimpse over our shoulders as we ran down the hill, they had begun to gather together in a single ominous knot.

And for the rest of that weekend, though of course we never talked about it in front of our parents, all we could think of, both boys and girls, was what was going to happen at school that coming week.

The first thing, clearly evident by recess on Monday morning, was that the boys had decided not to let us girls field at softball any more.

Softball at our school used to go like this: every Monday morning at recess two of the bigger boys—that year it was usually Ernie Chapman and Junior LeBlanc—used to pick their teams for the week. Whoever came out on top in laddering hands up the softball bat got to pick first and the loser second and so it went—back and forth—until all the boys who were considered good enough to be on a team had been picked. Then Ernie and Junior laddered the bat again to see which side would get up first and the losing side took to the field to be joined by the little boys who hadn't been picked and us older girls who were allowed to act as sort of permanent supplementary fielders. And for the rest of the week the teams remained locked, at every recess and lunchtime, in one long softball game which had, as we discovered to our surprise several years later when the television came through, some strange rules.

The way we played, for example, every single boy had to get out before the other team could come in. And any boy hitting a home run not only had the right to bat straight away again but also to bring back into the game any boy who had got out. Which led to kids who couldn't remember their six-times table properly being able to announce—say, by noon on Thursday—"The score's now 46 to 39 because, in the last inning starting Tuesday lunchtime, Junior's team was all out except for Irving Snell, who hit three homers in a row off of Lorne Ripley, and brought in Ira and Jim and Elton who brought in the rest except for Austin who got out for the second time on

Wednesday with a foul ball one of the girls caught behind third base . . ."

Some days it got so exciting that at noon we couldn't wait to eat our lunches but would rush straight into the schoolyard, gobbling our sandwiches as we ran, toward that aching moment when the ball, snaking across the yellow grass or arching toward us from the marsh sky, might meet our open, eager hands.

So it was a hard blow, Monday morning recess, when Ernie Chapman whirled the bat around his head, slammed it down as hard as he could on home base and announced, "The first girl that goes out to field, *we break her neck*." We clustered forlornly around the girls' entry door knowing there was nothing we could really do.

"Oh Alma," mourned Minnie Halliday, biting the ends of her long, brown braids, "why couldn't you just have kept your mouth shut?" It was a bad moment. If we'd tried to go out to field they'd have picked us off one by one. We couldn't even play softball on our own. None of us owned a bat and ball.

If it hadn't been for Doris Pomeroy, we might have broken rank right there and then. Doris, who was in Grade 9 and had had a home permanent and sometimes wore nail polish and had even, it was rumored, gone swimming in the quarry all alone with Elton Lawrence, flicked a rock against the schoolhouse wall in the silence following Minnie's remark and steadied us all by saying: "Don't be foolish, Minnie. All we have to do is wait. They need us to field and, besides, they kind of like to have us out there looking at them when they get up to bat."

But it was a long, hard week. Besides not letting us field, the boys picked on us whenever they got the chance. I guess they figured that if they made things bad enough for us, sooner or later we'd go to Miss Ralston and ask her to forget the whole thing. But all their picking on and bullying did was to keep us together. Whenever one of us was tripped going down the aisle or got an ink ball in her hair or got trapped in the outhouse by a bunch of boys it was as if it was happening to all of us. And looking back on that week—when there were so many bad feelings and so many new feelings in the air—it was kind of nice, too, because for the first time us girls found ourselves telling each other our troubles and even our thoughts without worrying about being laughed at. And that was something new at our school.

As for Alma, who kept getting notes thrown on her desk promising her everything from a bloody nose to having her pants pulled down, we stuck to her like burrs. But maybe Alma's hardest moment had nothing to do with bullying at all. It was when her cousin Arnold came over to see her Wednesday after school and asked her to drop the whole idea of girls going for the water.

"If they find out about it, Alma," said Arnold, "they'll probably take away the water bucket."

"Who's they?" asked Alma. She and Arnold had played a lot together when they were little kids and she was used to listening to his opinions on most things.

"Well, the health inspector," said Arnold, "and guys like that."

"They'll never take away that water bucket," said Alma, though she wasn't all that sure. "They don't care who carries the water as long as it gets carried."

"Alma," said Arnold earnestly, "the other guys would kill me if they ever found out I told you this but sometimes carrying the water isn't that much fun. On cold days it's real hard work. You're better off in the warm school."

Alma knew what it cost Arnold to tell her this but she stood firm. "I'm sorry, Arnold," she said, "but I'm used to cold weather. In winter I walk to school the same as you." So Arnold went away.

If Miss Ralston, as the week wore on, noticed anything unusual going on in her school, she gave little sign of it. She passed out the usual punishments for ink balls, she intercepted threatening notes and tore them up unread, she looked at Alma's white face, and all she asked about were the principal rivers of Europe. Nor were we surprised. Nothing in our experience had led us to believe the grown-ups had the slightest inkling—or interest—in what really went on with kids.

Only Doris Pomeroy thought differently. "Miss Ralston looks real mad," said Doris as we trailed in thankfully from Friday morning recess.

"Mad?" a couple of us asked.

"Yeah. Like when she comes out to ring the bell and we're all hanging around the entry door like a lot of scared chickens. She rings that old handbell as if she wished all those yelling boys' heads were under it. Of course they do things differently in River Hibbert. I know for a fact that girls there get to play on softball teams just like the boys."

"On teams? Just like the boys?" But it was all too much for us to take in at that moment, so preoccupied were we with that afternoon's decision on the water. All that long, hard week it was as if Friday afternoon and Junior Red Cross would never come again. Now that it was almost upon us most of us forgot, in our excitement, at least for the time being, Doris' heady remark about softball.

So at lunchtime, just as the boys were winding up their week's game ("And real great, eh? Without the girls?" Ernie Chapman was gloating loudly from the pitcher's mound), when Miss Ralston, without her bell, leaped through our clustered huddles at the entry door and headed straight toward the softball field, she took us all completely by surprise. Crunch, crunch, crunch went Miss Ralston's bright red loafers against the cinders and the next thing we knew she'd grabbed the bat from Irving Snell and, squinting against the sun, was twirling and lining it before our astonished eyes.

"Come on! Come on!" cried Miss Ralston impatiently to Ernie who stood transfixed before her on the pitcher's mound. "Come on! Come on!" she cried again and she banged the bat against the ground.

"Come on! Come on!" cried Doris Pomeroy and we rushed after her across the cinders.

The first ball Ernie threw was pretty wobbly and Miss Ralston hit it at an angle so that it fell sideways, a foul ball, toward George Fowler's outstretched hands. "Ah-h-h-h-h," we moaned from the sidelines and some of us closed our eyes so we wouldn't have to look. But George jumped too eagerly for such an easy ball and it fell right through his fingers and rolled harmlessly along the ground.

Ernie took a lot more time over his second pitch. He was getting over the first shock of finding Miss Ralston opposite him at bat and by this time he was receiving shouts of encouragement from all over the field.

"Get her! Get her!" the boys yelled recklessly at Ernie and they all fanned out behind the bases.

Ernie took aim slowly. None of us had ever seen the pirouettings of professional pitchers but there was a certain awesome ceremony, nevertheless, as Ernie spat savagely on the ball, glared hard at Miss Ralston, slowly swung back his big right arm and, poised for one long moment, his whole body outstretched, threw the ball as hard as he could toward home base where Miss Ralston waited, her body rocking with the bat.

For a fleeting moment we had a glimpse of what life

might be like in River Hibbert and then Miss Ralston hit the ball.

"Ah-h-h-h-h-h," we cried as it rose high in the air, borne by the marsh wind, and flew like a bird against the sun, across the road and out of sight, into the ox pasture on the other side.

"Ah-h-h-h-h-h . . ."

We all stared at Miss Ralston. "School's in," she announced over her shoulder, walking away. Hitting the ball into the ox pasture happened maybe once a year.

That afternoon, toward the end of Red Cross, there was a big hush all over the room.

"Next week," said Miss Ralston, closing the school register, tidying her books, "next week Alma Niles and Joyce Shipley will go for the water."

She swept her hand over the top of her desk and tiny dust motes danced in the slanting sun.

About the Authors

Arnold Adoff is an anthologist and children's poet who was born in New York in 1935. As a white teacher in New York, he became frustrated with the lack of black literature available for his students. He decided to compile and edit his own anthologies, which have received numerous awards. He also writes poetry for young people.

Bob Arnold, born in 1952, is a lumberyard worker, carpenter, and stonemason from New England, who has also published several collections of poetry. He claims that splitting firewood is what brings the first line of a poem to his mind.

Leslie Gordon Barnard (1890–1961) was from Montréal. He wrote short stories and radio scripts and also won the Québec Government Award for Fiction in 1940 for his book *Jancia.*

Walter Bauer (1904–1976) wrote over 60 books in a variety of forms and on numerous topics. He was a poet, novelist, short story writer, biographer, essayist, and dramatist. He also taught in German public schools for 10 years and, when he moved to Canada in 1952, taught German at the University of Toronto.

Sandra Cisneros was born in Chicago, the daughter of a Mexican father and a Mexican-American mother. She has worked as a teacher, college recruiter, and an arts administrator, and she travels to schools across the country as a visiting writer. Her work has been translated into seven languages.

Robert Cormier, a novelist, was born in 1925 in Massachusetts. All of his young adult novels have been named Best Books of the Year by the American Library Association, and two of them have been made into movies. He has also written novels for adults and has been a newspaper writer and editor.

Richard Davies was born in Winnipeg, Manitoba, in 1949. He teaches English at Strathcona Composite High School in Edmonton, Alberta. Author of 25 high school textbooks and teachers' guides, he has also published more than 100 poems. He often reads his poetry with an Edmonton performance group called Spiritus.

Borden Deal was born in 1922 and writes books that provide, in his words, "a panorama of the New South" in the United States. He likes to show what people in the South are doing and thinking now, apart from the historic past of their region. He has contributed over 100 stories, poems, and reviews to national magazines.

John Donne experienced both extreme wealth and extreme poverty before becoming an Anglican priest in England. He is considered a prominent poet of the seventeenth century, although none of his poetry collections were published until after he died.

China Galland has worked as a river guide and university lecturer and is the mother of three. Her book *Women in the Wilderness* investigates women's relationship to the wilderness throughout history and profiles women adventurers of the past and present.

Leona Gom has been a secretary, waitress, tombstone cutter, and teacher at all grade levels. She has published poetry and a novel.

Anne Hart grew up in Nova Scotia. She has written short stories and poetry for Canadian magazines, as well as two fictional biographies about Agatha Christie's detectives. Hart works as a librarian at Memorial University of Newfoundland.

Tod Hartje is currently playing for the minor-league club of the Winnipeg Jets in Moncton, New Brunswick.

Carol Kleiman lives in Illinois. Her article "My Home Is Not Broken, It Works," from which the anthology selection is excerpted, appeared in *Ms.* magazine in November 1984.

Karla Kuskin was born and grew up in New York City. She writes illustrated poetry books for children.

Alonzo Lopez is a Papago from Arizona. Although his major interests are writing and poetry, he also works in drama, dance, and traditional Native American crafts.

Lawrence Martin, once the Russian correspondent for the *Globe and Mail,* is now working on his fourth book, about Canadian–U.S. relations.

Lisa Moore, born in Ohio in 1955, has been writing poetry since she was in high school. She taught English for 10 years, and she now is a full-time writer of poetry, short stories, novels, and textbooks.

K. Reed Needles, born in 1953 in Toronto, is a drama teacher, actor, director, musician, and storyteller for all ages. He tells fiction and non-fiction tales at festivals, schools, libraries, and parties. "Laura and the Lilies," based on an event from his childhood, was originally included in one of his oral performances.

Susin Nielsen, who was born in 1964, began writing when she was 16 years old. By age 22 she was already writing for the award-winning television series *Degrassi Junior High.* She continues to work on documentaries, soap operas, and television dramas.

Harry Paddon grew up in Labrador, where he spent much of his adult life working as a trapper. He lives in British Columbia and writes stories for books and magazines.

Aleck Paul was a Chippewa who lived with the Temagami band at Bear Island, Ontario, at the turn of the twentieth century. His account was recorded by the anthropologist Frank G. Speck, who included

Paul's story in a 1915 speech at the University of Pennsylvania about the Aboriginal land ownership controversy.

Al Purdy, born in 1918 in Wooler, Ontario, has written and edited scores of poetry books. A factory worker until 1960, Purdy began publishing his poetry at the age of 26. He has also contributed to CBC radio and television programs.

Paul Simon was born in 1942 in New Jersey. Part of the popular duo Simon and Garfunkel from 1964 to 1971, he later began producing albums of his own. He has won a number of Grammy Awards for his songs.

Mary B. Smith won a short story contest with "Alfred the Great." A schoolteacher for 37 years, she lives in Pennsylvania with her husband. Her short story is the first fiction she has written.

Paul Yee enjoys writing because he says it can help to make people and their stories endure. He writes mostly about the people he knows best, Chinese Canadians. Born in 1956 in Spalding, Saskatchewan, Yee has published four books.

Vytaute Zilinskaite is a Lithuanian writer who was born in 1930. She writes poetry, satirical stories, short novels, and books for children. Twice she has won the State Prize of Lithuania for her work.

Credits

11 "Laura and the Lilies" by K. Reed Needles. Reprinted by permission of the author.

16 From WOMAN HOLLERING CREEK. Copyright © Sandra Cisneros 1991. Published by Vintage Books, a division of Random House, Inc., New York and simultaneously in Canada by Random House Canada Limited, Toronto. Originally published in hardcover by Random House, Inc. in 1991. Reprinted by permission of Susan Bergholz Literary Services, New York.

18 From *Lost Not Missing: Poems of Prairie Boyhood* by Spiritus, © 1990. Reprinted with permission of the author.

20 From *Green Woods and Blue Waters* by Harry Paddon. Copyright © 1989 by Harry Paddon. By permission of Breakwater Books Ltd., St. John's, Newfoundland.

27 Reprinted from *Literary Cavalcade* magazine. Copyright © 1954 by Scholastic Inc. Used with permission. All rights reserved.

34 From THE CHOCOLATE WAR by Robert Cormier. Copyright © 1974 by Robert Cormier. Reprinted by permission of Pantheon Books, a division of Random House, Inc.

41 "Alfred the Great" by Mary B. Smith. Reprinted by permission of the author.

50 Excerpt from "Body Politics" written by Susin Nielsen for the series *Degrassi High*. Created by Linda Schuyler and Kit Hood and produced by Playing With Time, Inc.

68 From SPORTS PAGES by Arnold Adoff. Text copyright © 1986 by Arnold Adoff. Selection reprinted by permission of HarperCollins Publishers.

69 "Antaeus" by Borden Deal reprinted by permission of Ashley Deal Moss.

83 Appeared in *Face to Face: A Collection of Stories by Celebrated Soviet and American Writers*, edited by Thomas Pettepiece and Anatoly Aleksin. Copyright © 1990 by Thomas Pettepiece and Anatoly Aleksin.

94 From *Women in the Wilderness* by China Galland. Copyright © 1980 by China Galland.

98 Appeared in *Poetry East* magazine, no. 32. Copyright © 1991 by Poetry East, Dept. of English, De Paul University, Chicago, IL.

99 Appeared in *Inquiry into Literature 4*, Collier Macmillan Canada, Inc.

100 "Perspective" by Leona Gom from The Collected Poems, Sono Nis Press.

101 Reprinted with the permission of Macmillan Publishing Company from FROM BEHIND THE RED LINE: AN AMERICAN HOCKEY PLAYER IN RUSSIA by Tod Hartje with Lawrence Martin. Copyright © 1992 by Tod Hartje and Lawrence Martin.

105 Excerpt from "Meditation 17" by John Donne.